Gloria Pitzer!

Secret Ingredients

Dear Friends

PURE INSPIRATION! That's what these recipes are made of. Each one of the nearly 400 recipes in this book have been inspired by a dish or product of a famous restaurant or grocery shelf food item. In developing each of these Make-Alikes I have had only the product as a guide. I do not know, nor do I want to know what the famous food people put into their foods. I do know, however, that by combining the compatible ingredients in our recipes, we can come up with Make-Alikes that will remind you of the original dish which we attempt here to imitate.

The Recipe Detective

more than just a passing fancy

TASTE TESTING:

SECRET INGREDIENTS in these recipes are probably unique when compared to traditional recipes for similar dishes, but I look for ingredients that are available, economical and wholesome. When possible I reduce the number of ingredients by using a prepared product in place of several other ingredients.

Gloria Pitzer's MAKE ALIKE RECIPES

AUTHOR'S NOTE

SEPT-1994

THE WORLD, it is said, is divided into 2 kinds of cooks. Those who thrive on the personal inner rewards from being good at it, and those who regard it as an occupational hazard.

THIS BOOK is for the cook who finds the experience one that must be endured with a minimum of effort and still achieve a maximum result!

IF COOKING means to you, a series of achievements from which derive great personal satisfaction and continuous compliments, you may be excused from this explanation and forge at once ahead into the recipe portion of this book. The rest of you, please pay attention. You are about to find reassurance that cooking can be accomplished with confidence. When you are not an exceptional cook, you can muddle through the murky waters of an offshore success, hoping that one dish will come along to prompt a little praise, and with a little practice, more praise. But when cooking doesn't come easily to you, the search for a successful recipe continues, cookbook after cookbook.

THIS ONE PROMISES to be different!

It is like my other books, but the recipes are different. I try not to repeat recipes from one book to the other, with the exception of the pie crust, perhaps a salad dressing we use often, or another recipe you will need without having to consult another book that you may not have. There are about 300 recipes in this book, although I haven't really counted them and feel that "a pearl of great price" should not be compared to a bargain basement book in any manner since the recipes in this book are truly unique! These are what I consider the best possible imitations of the famous dishes and grocery shelf products you can find today. I must clear it up right now (and I am constantly telling their lawyers this) that I do not KNOW what these companies put into their dishes — nor do I WANT to know, since you have only to take my recipes and the possibly unlikely ingredients I have used, to find you have a practically perfect "make alike" version of theirs. In most cases you can adjust the ingredients to accomodate your specific concerns, such as Land O Lake's "light" butter for real butter, Egg Beaters for real eggs, unless I specifically tell you NOT to tamper with a recipe. Use less salt if that's your choice, as well. Customize the recipes, please!

BECAUSE COOKING has always been exploited as an art based on a science, many reluctantly back away from a recipe with more than 5 or 6 ingredients or a dozen sentences of instructions on how to put those ingredients together. It's like trying to drive a car without ever having to turn a corner, or maneuver into a tight parking place, or back out of a driveway into heavy traffic. Even with cooking, we have to know, if only by instinct, or impulse, what we should do when the recipe we're using doesn't completely suit us. The secreet of GOOD cooking, is nicely confined to one technique - timing! When you can anticipate how long a particular step in a recipe will take, you can pretty well determine when to start a 2nd or 3rd or 4th dish in a meal, so that everything is going to be ready to serve at the same time. So naturally you begin with the dish that requires the longest time to prepare and end with the dish that requires the least amount of time.

In between you set the table, attend to the beverages, making sure that the little items are on the table and handy for the last few minutes before everyone sits down to enjoy the meal.

LIKE MY FAVORITES RESTAURANTS, you'll notice in this collection that I have included some favorite recipes from friends who row the same boat with me down the river of reluctance when mealtime boredom sets in. We are tired of the same old standbys, had our fill of being scared into counting every gram of fat, every mouthful of cholesterol, and we are looking now for some wisdom, intelligent choices, moderation and above all wholesome enjoyment in both preparation and presentation.

IN MOST OF MY RECIPES, with the exception of delicate cakes that might fall or shrink, you can, if fat is a concern to you, substitute Land O Lakes new product called "light" butter, which they say has 50% the fat of real butter. It does not seem to affect most of my cooked sauces, sauteed dishes, but when using in in cookies, I compensate for the dryness it will cause by using for every 1/2-lb of "light" butter, a 4-oz jar of Heinz babyfood apricots with tapioca. I have tested numerous possibilities and by accident, one day this proved to be the best for moist flavorful results. With salad dressings feel free to use the new "light" products unless I say not to.

Gloria Pitzer's MAKE ALIKE RECIPES

Signs Of The Times

THERE'S ALWAYS ROOM FOR ONE MORE GOOD RESTAURANT — ONE MORE GOOD FOOD IDEA!

Culinary Concepts — The places known for good food

If it ain't broke, don't fix it

IN THE MIDST OF SIMPLICITY and modest efficiency, Paul and I and our family have provided SECRET RECIPES to people all over the world. We've been doing what we do, the way we do it, since 1973. And people keep coming to us over the years asking if there isn't a better way, a state of the arts way to update or improve what we're doing & how we do it. Without so much as spending an entire day with us as we work, we've had suggestions & directives made with all good intentions as to how we might change our production techniques, but if it was good enough for McDonald's, simplicity is good enough for us, or as Grandpa would insist: "If it ain't broke, don't fix it."

Good taste runs in our family.
To keep you posted on what's going on

The surge of mail that we received after Kelly & Co TV Show was followed quickly by mail from the viewers of Buffalo's Channel 7 showing of our recipes being prepared on their AM Show. An average day in our work includes Paul and I opening, reading and replying to anywhere from 600-to-1,000 letters. Whenever a subscription or book order comes in with an accompanying question or recipe request, that question or request gets our first attention and priority. There just isn't enough time to answer every question & request that the general public will ask of us, and as much as I would like to be in what is called "missionary work", we can only offer the public the sheet of 15 of our most requested recipes as samples of what our books and newsletters include. We don't have a secretary or a staff to assist us in our work, so when I am given the invitation to seek out a certain restaurant or product and try to duplicate it, it all depends on a number of things, the distance we have to travel, the cost involved, the time we have available. With over 30 different radio broadcasts around the country each month, our investigations take time to cover. But sooner or later we will cover these if at all possible. I regret I cannot accept individual assignments.

Gloria Pitzer's MAKE ALIKE RECIPES

WHOLE WHEAT BREAD Inspired by Schafer's

In lg bowl stir together 4 cups whole wheat flour, ½-cup packed light brown sugar, 2 TB granulated sugar, 2 pkgs dry yeast, 1 TB salt. Set aside. In saucepan heat to lukewarm, 1½-cups water, 3/4-cup milk, ¼-cup margarine. Pour into flour mixture, beating with mixer on med-speed till smooth. Remove beaters. Work in 1½ to 2 cups all-purpose flour with spoon to smooth dough. Dip kneading hand into ½-cup more flour & knead dough in bowl till smooth & elastic & no longer sticky. Place dough in lg greased bowl or Dutch oven. Turn dough to grease surface. Cover with loose sheet Saran Wrap, greased on down side. In 90 mins dough should be doubled. Punch down. Pat out into 2 rectangles 9x12" & roll up 9" side to press out bubbles. Fit these into 2 greased 9" loaf pans. Bake at 350F 35-40 mins or till golden brown, or till crust makes hollow sound when tapped with fingers. (Bake center rack of oven). Turn baked bread out of pans at once to cool on sides of loaves on rack 4 hrs before slicing. Makes 2.

Something this good Shouldn't be so easy
Cheese Biscuits right on the money

GARLIC CHEESE BISCUITS Inspired by Red Lobster's

Combine in 1½-qt mixing bowl, 1 cup milk, 1/3-cup mayonnaise, 1 TB sugar (or 3 packets Sweet & Low) 2 cups self-rising flour, using wire whisk till you have a smooth thick batter. Then work in 1/2-cup more self-rising flour sufficient to give you a dough you can DROP by spoon & it holds it shape without spreading. Streak dough to marbleize with about 1/4-cup KRAFT'S GRATED AMERICAN CHEESE FOOD (powdered) or finely shredded Cheddar (but powdered is best & comes in gold cylinder like their Parmesan). Drop batter 1" apart into 9 equal mounds on Pam-sprayed jelly roll pan. spray top of each in a bit of Pam & dust with pinch more powdered cheese. Then bake at 350F- 25 to 30 mins or till golden brown. Right out of oven dust in garlic salt & serve promptly. Makes 9 (Do not add too much flour to dough or biscuits will bake up hard.)

Gloria Pitzer's MAKE ALIKE RECIPES

GRAPENUTS CEREAL PEBBLES

- 4 cups rye flour
- 2 cups packed brown sugar
- 1 tsp salt
- 1 tsp baking soda
- 1 egg
- ½-cup dark molasses
- 1½-cups buttermilk

Combine flour, sugar, salt, soda and mix thoroughly in medium-sized bowl. Combine the egg, molasses and buttermilk in blender on high speed about 1 minute. Make a well in center of flour mixture and pour in the liquid mixture, working it into a smooth dough. Spread the dough no more than ½" deep in greased jelly roll pans, and bake at 250F—(very low) about 2 hours or till thoroughly dried. Cool in pan about 10 minutes. Dump it out and break up mixture, crushing into pebble sized pieces with rolling pin or hammer. Store in covered containers at room temperature to use within 4 or 5 months. Makes about 1-lb.

Special Recipe

CINNAMON BREAD Inspired by HOWARD JOHNSON'S RESTAURANT

- ¼-cup warm water
- 1 TB sugar
- 2 pkgs dry yeast
- 1½-cups Borden's canned eggnog
- 3½-cups all-purpose flour

Combine water, sugar & yeast in measuring cup. Stir once or twice just 5to combine. Let stand 5 mins or till bubbly. Meanwhile beat eggnog with **1 cup of flour** till smooth & beat in yeast mixture, then only 2 more cups of flour. Leave the rest for kneading later. Cover dough with inverted bowl same size as bowl containing dough, having greased inside of top bowl. Let it rest 15 mins. Now dip kneading hand into remaining flour & work it into dough, kneading it right in that bowl till smooth & elastic. Dump dough into greased bowl. Invert another greased bowl same size over it so you can see how it's doing as it rises for about 90 mins in warm place - till doubled. Punch dough down. Pat out on waxed paper to 9" lonbg rectangle. Wipe surface of dough lightly in a little melted butter or margarine & dust lightly in a mixture of **1 TB sugar + 1 tsp cinnamon.** Roll up jelly roll style & place seam side down in 9" bread loaf pan. Let rise in warm place till doubled in bulk. Bake by placing in COLD oven & setting temp at 425F- for only **8 mins** - reducing temp at once to 350F-to bake another 30 mins or till well browned & crust makes "hollow" sound when thumped with your fingers. Immediately remove bread from pan to wire rack, placing loaf on side to cool. For a soft crust, wipe top in a little melted butter or margariner. Do not attempt to slice bread for at least **4 hours.** Makes 1 loaf.

...the way we make bread.

Gloria Pitzer's MAKE ALIKE RECIPES

SOFT BREADSTICKS CRAZY BREAD

THE PERFECT PIZZA DOUGH

PIZZA ROLLS or what Little Caesar's calls their "Crazy Bread" is also like the rolls served at Chuck Muer Restaurants. To re-create these at home, begin with prepared pizza dough from any of our recommended recipes. Let the dough rise, as each recipe will direct, in a greased bowl, in a warm place, till doubled—usually with another bowl the same diameter, also greased inside, inverted over the bowl of dough while rising. Punch down that doubled dough and break off pieces about the size of an egg. Pat out to a rectangle shape, keeping it ½" thick. Roll the dough into cigar shapes and arrange 1" apart on greased and cornmeal dusted jelly roll pans. Wipe the top of each with slightly beaten egg white and sprinkle in Kosher Salt and a little garlic powder. OR instead of Kosher Salt and garlic powder, let rolls rise till doubled on the baking sheet and bake at 375F—about 16 to 18 mins or till golden brown and as soon as they're out of the oven, wipe tops lightly with a little bottled Italian Salad Dressing and then sprinkle in Kosher Salt. Frozen store-bought bread dough can be thawed and shaped as described above and baked into Pizza Rolls as well. There are also small loaf tube can doughs in the dairy section of the supermarket that can be shaped and baked as I have just described, rather than making your own from scratch!

PIZZA

ICE BOX PIZZA DOUGH

Keep the prepared dough in a plastic food bag in the refrigerator to use within a week. Or pat it out promptly over the pizza pans & freeze them to use within 3 months.

¼-cup lukewarm water
2 TB sugar
1 pkg dry yeast
2 tsp salt
1 cup Tonic Water
3 cups Pillsbury's Bread Flour or all-purpose flour

In 2½-qt mixing bowl stir 1st 3 ingredients a few times. Let stand 5 mins or till bubbly. Stir in each remaining ingredient, working in the flour with your hands till dough is smooth, elastic and not the least bit sticky to the touch. Shape into smooth ball & let rise in greased 3-quart bowl with piece of greased waxed paper, greased side down, covering the bowl. When doubled in size (1½-hrs approx), punch down. Refrigerate in plastic food bags, tightly secured with wire twists or tape, to roll out & bake within a week. OR stretch the dough with your hands to fit greased & cornmeal dusted pizza pans, so that dough is ¼" thick. Brush lightly in oil & dust in Parmesan cheese & freeze in plastic bags to thaw & fill & bake within 3 months. Makes three 15" crusts.

PIZZA FLAT BREAD

Prepare the dough exactly as directed above, but after the last rising, divide into 4 equal portions & shape into rounds to fit greased & cornmeal dusted 9" pie pans. Let rise till doubled. Wipe surface of each with a beaten egg diluted with 1 TB cold water. Sprinkle each with sesame seeds or dust lightly in oregano leaves and a bit of garlic salt & then coarse salt. Place on lowest rack of a preheated 475F—oven for 5 minutes & transfer pans to highest rack of oven, reducing heat to 425F—for another 15 minutes or till well browned and puffy. Remove at once from pans. Store in plastic bags at room temperature to use within a week or freeze to use in 3 months. Makes four 9" rounds.

Gloria Pitzer's MAKE ALIKE RECIPES

Breadsticks
Inspired by Olive Garden's

BEST KEPT SECRET GARLIC BREAD

LIKE CHARLIE'S UPTOWN AS WELL!!!

Begin with a loaf of frozen unbaked bread, allowing it to thaw at room temperature in a greased large mixing bowl. When it's soft enough to knead, spray your fingers with a little bit of Pam or oil & knead dough just till you can shape it into cigar-sized pieces. Place these 3" apart on Pam-sprayed cookie sheets. Let rise in warm place till doubled — about 1½ hours. Then holding can of Pam about 8" from bread sticks, lightly spray top of each & then dust each in just a bit of garlic powder & dry oregano leaf rubbed to a dust between your fingers. Bake these at 375F- about 20 to 25 mins or till golden brown. Cool in pan on rack to serve within a day or two. Makes about 8 to 10.

Less Work

SELF RISING FLOUR
2 cups all-purpose flour
1 TB baking powder
1 tsp salt

Sift together these ingredients, 4 times. Recipe may be cut in half. Makes about 2 cups.

BILL NAPKIN'S BUTTERY BISCUIT ROLLS

When you try to imitate the product of the well-known dinner house it requires some attention in the time allowed for the dough to rise. Other than that—it's a snap!

¼-cup lukewarm water
1 envelope dry yeast
1 tsp sugar

2/3 cup warm water
¼-lb butter, melted
1 beaten egg
1 TB baking powder
1 tsp salt
4 cups flour

Stir the ¼-cup warm water, dry yeast and the 1 tsp sugar together in small bowl or measuring cup. Let it stand 5 or 6 mins or till bubbly and doubled in bulk. Meanwhile beat the remaining warm water with melted butter, egg and baking powder and salt. Beat in half of the flour, then the yeast mixture and work in last 2 cups of flour to a smooth dough that can be kneaded in the bowl with lightly floured hands till no longer sticky. Shape the dough into smooth ball and place in greased 2-qt bowl, turning dough to grease the top. Invert another bowl —greased inside— same size, over bowl of dough & let rise till doubled—about 1 hour. Punch down & knead in the bowl a few times. Shape again into smooth ball and again let rise till doubled, with inverted bowl same size covering bowl of dough. When doubled again, shape dough into patties 1" thick and about 4" around. Wipe top of each with just a bit of soft butter and fold each patty in half, placing them close together in greased 9" square baking pan. Wipe tops of these with —an egg beaten well with 1 tsp water. Let rise till biscuits are doubled in size. Bake at 375F—about 30 to 35 minutes or till nicely golden and lightly browned. Cool rolls in pan about 30 mins before serving. Makes about 9 large biscuit-rolls.

Gloria Pitzer's MAKE ALIKE RECIPES

Try These For Starters

SOURDOUGH STARTER FOR FRIENDSHIP CAKE

The idea is basically the same with all 3 of these traditional starters. The fermentation of each is caused by the sugar in each of the mixtures combined with the warm temperature in which it is kept.

The container in which you will store each of the starters should NOT be metal. I suggest a 1-gallon plastic beverage container with a tight fitting lid that has a small hole in the top through which to pour out the beverage the jug is intended to contain. While fermenting the starter batter in one of these jugs, you can leave the small pouring hole uncapped, allowing just enough air to get at the starter, as will be required to make it "work" or bubble.

FRIENDSHIP FRUIT STARTER

Combine canned fruits "in heavy syrup", with equal amount of sugar, stirring well, 4 or 5 times a day for several days, keeping in warm-ish place, covered as described above—until sugar completely dissolves. For every 6 cups of the mixture, sprinkle 1 pkg dry yeast over it and stir it in — using only plastic or wooden stirring utensils—never metal. Allow to ferment at room temperature, bubbling till mixture has an aroma like beer, alcoholic, then capping it tightly and refrigerating it to use as specific recipe directs (to follow). Replacement of starter is again — equal parts canned fruits, sliced Cling peaches, fruit cocktain, pineapple chunks, green grapes, pears) and granulated sugar, prepared as above. If you remove 1½-cups starter, you must mix together ¾-cup canned (undrained) fruits plus ¾-cup sugar, to equal 1½-cups.

FRIENDSHIP CAKE BATTER:

In large bowl combine 18-oz box yellow cake mix, 4-serving size box instant vanilla pudding powder, ¾-cup oil, 4 eggs, beating till smooth, using electric mixer, medium-high speed. Beat in 1½-cups drained fruit starter, 1 cup finely chopped pecans or walnuts. Turn into greased, floured 12-cup Bundt pan. Bake center rack of 350F— oven, 1 hour—or till paper-covered, wire trash bag "twist" inserted into center of baked poortion of cake, comes out clean. Cool upright in pan on wire rack 45 mins. Loosen edges of cake with tip of sharp knife. Invert onto platter. Drizzle cake in Thin Vanilla Icing (Index).

POTATO FLAKES STARTER (For Sourdough—or Herman)

Combine in small cup—¼-cup warm water, 1 tsp sugar, 1 pkg dry yeast, stirring once or ttwice. Let stand 5 mins or till bubbly. In large mixing bowl beat together with electric mixer, medium speed, 2 cups warm water, 1 cup boxed potato flakes or "Buds", 2 cups flour, 2 cups sugar. When smooth, beat in yeast mixture. Turn into plastic 1-gallon juice container as described above. Allow to stand with pouring hole uncapped, room temperature, 3 days or till mixture has a strong sour aroma, almost alcoholic in smell.

POTATO STARTER RAISIN BREAD

Combine 1 cup Potato Starter, 3 TB oil, 1 cup flour, ¼-tsp baking soda, ¼-tsp salt, till you can knead dough with your hand, right in bowl. Dip hand into just enough flour that dough becomes smooth & elastic, no longer sticky. Use back of floured mixing spoon if you wish with which to knead dough, kneading into the dough: ½-cup "plumped" raisins drained & dusted lightly in ½-tsp cinnamon, 3 TB sugar. Shape dough into 12 equally sized balls. Dust each ball evenly in a mixture of 3 TB sugar plus 1 tsp cinnamon. Drop balls into greased 1-quart baking dish. Let rise in dish till doubled in size. Bake at 425F— 25 mins or till golden brown. Soon as out of oven, drizzle top of loaf with Thin Vanill Icing. (See Index). Cool in dish on rack before cutting into wedges to serve 6 senibly or 2 foolishly!

For all starters except fruit starter use replacement recipe given with San Francisco recipe page 11...

Ours doesn't have to take hours.

Gloria Pitzer's MAKE ALIKE RECIPES

My experiences with the recipes now circulating for the Herman Starter have proven to be time consuming and bothersome inasmuch as each required a 10-day fermentation period before it could be incorporated into baking recipes. After 3 days of continuous tests to develop our own that would be ready in one day, I came across a mixture that truly pleased us, and the many friends we have been sharing it with. I was so absorbed with this challange that I even got out of bed at 3 a.m. once to experiment with an idea that wouldn't let me sleep. The natural cultures in dairy buttermilk made the difference, producing a quick-acting batter that needed no refrigeration, as did the others, was easily handled with a single basic mixture and produced an excellent flavor and texture. It will keep for weeks without being used, if you will just remember to stir it once a day or even once every other day, just to let Herman know you care!

SAN FRANCISCO SOURDOUGH (Herman)

1 pkg dry yeast
¼-cup warm water
1 tsp sugar
2 cups dairy buttermilk
2 cups flour
2 cups sugar

Soften yeast in water with sugar. Stir once or twice. Let stand 5 mins or till doubled in volume. (If it doesn't double & bubble, the yeast is no good. Throw it out & start over with a fresh packet.)
Beat remaining 3 ingredients together till smooth & beat in the bubbly yeast mixture at end of the 5 mins. Pour into non-metal 8-cup container with a loose fitting lid. Let stand in warm place 6 hours. As it bubbles up, stir it down (after 2nd or 3rd hour, so don't be impatient!) Then it is ready to use. Say hello to Herman! Just remember to keep Herman out of drafts. Set him in a sunny spot, once in awhile. He delights in this! He'll bubble up with excitement if the sun's shining on him awhile! Now pay attention to the "replacement" recipe, please.

THE REPLACEMENT RECIPE FOR HERMAN

Everytime you remove a cup of Herman to incorporate into a specific recipe, you must replace him at once with a simple mixture of:

1 cup water   1 cup flour   1 cup sugar

Beat it smooth and stir it into the mixture from which you removed the cupful for baking purposes. The above 3-cup mixture makes 1 cup of starter batter exactly, once the sugar is reduced to liquids and the flour settles into a paste with the water. If you remove TWO cups of the starter to use in a recipe, double the above replacement ingredients. Always leave at least one cup of the starter at all times with which to begin your next batch of Herman Starter.

SOURDOUGH BISCUITS (Herman Biscuits)

1 cup starter
3 TB oil
1 cup flour
¼-tsp baking soda
¼-tsp salt

Combine ingredients with large sturdy spoon coated lightly in flour, using it to knead the dough with the back of this floured spoon, until dough is no longer sticky. Then flour the palms of your hands & make a patty of the dough, kneading it between the palsm of your hands about 10 times. Divide dough into 6 equal pieces. Shape into 1" thick patties. Arrange in greased 1-qt baking dish or pan and bake 425F— for 18 to 20 mins or till golden brown. Let cool in dish for 10 mins before serving. Makes 6 biscuits. Recipe may be doubled or tripled. (Don't forget to replace the starter with 1 portion of Replacement Recipe for each cup of Herman you removed.)

Gloria Pitzer's MAKE ALIKE RECIPES

HERMAN SOURDOUGH RAISIN BREAD

When you begin kneading the biscuit dough from the recipe on the preceding page, using the back of the floured spoon, work in the following ingredients:

½-tsp cinnamon
½-cup raisins
3 TB sugar

Continue kneading Herman biscuit dough between the palms of your hands as directed in Biscuit Recipe. Grease the 1-qt baking dish and break Herman up into 12 small balls. Dust each ball of biscuit dough in a mixture of:

3 TB sugar plus 1 tsp cinnamon

Drop the balls into the prepared baking dish and bake at 425F— about 20 to 23 mins or till golden. As soon as it is out of the oven, drizzle top with this icing:

THIN VANILLA GLAZE

½-cup powdered sugar
1 TB buttermilk
2 tsp melted butter
Few drops vanilla
Dash of salt

Beat on high speed with electric mixer till satin-smooth, or put everything through your blender on high speed till mixture is smooth. Makes about ½-cupful—just enough to glaze one 9" cake or the Raisin Bread

THE GOOD SAMARITAN COFFEECAKE

When you give away a cup of Herman a note must accompany it reading: "This is Herman. Treat him with love and keep him warm and away from drafts. Within 3 days of receiving this portion of his secret cake starter, please add to him, a smooth mixture of one cup each—water, flour and sugar. Let him stand in a non-metallic container with a loose-fitting lid for 6 hours before using a portion of him in the following recipe..."

1 cup Starter	½-cup buttermilk	½-tsp baking soda
1½-tsp baking powder	¼-lb butter, melted	1 cup sugar
3 large eggs	¼-tsp salt	2 cups flour
1 tsp vanilla	1 tsp orange extract	Dash nutmeg
	1 c chopped walnuts	1 cup raisins

Beat ingredients together as listed, beating well with each addition and 6 mins on med speed with last addition. Divide batter between two 9" greased foil cake pans, placed on cookie sheet positioned on center rack of oven. Bake at 350F— for 30 to 35 mins or till browned. Pierce each cake with tines of fork or toothpick in 20 or 30 places and drizzle at once with thinned vanilla icing, spreading each then with thin layer of Sweet Orange Marmalade, slightly warmed in small pan to pouring consistency. Sprinkle top with shredded coconut and place a thin slice of fresh orange in center of each cake for garnish. Wrap in foil and take one to a friend along with a cup of Herman and directions for adding to the starter and making your own. Keep one cake for yourself. They freeze well to be used within 6 months. (Makes two 9" cakes.)

Gloria Pitzer's MAKE ALIKE RECIPES — 13

VANILLA BLENDER ICING

1 tsp vanilla
2 TB light Karo syrup
4 TB margarine—softened
Dash of Salt
1/3 cup buttermilk
2 cups powdered sugar

As listed put all ingredients into blender, blending high speed half a minute or till smooty. Refrigerate unused icing, covered, to use in a 2 week period. Freeze to thaw & use within a year. Makes 1½-cups

Reliable McFABULOUS Apple Muffins

BREADS, BISCUITS AND MUFFINS

McDonald's World-Famous

The one recipe nobody ever asked for and once I tried this famous product, I could understand why. If I were serving a light, moist, tasty apple muffin, I would make it like so!

Beat together a 20-oz can apple pie filling, 3 eggs, 2 tsp apple pie spice & 18-oz box yellow cake mix (used dry right from the box). When all ingredients are completely moistened, but over-beaten, I would divide the batter equally between 24 paper lined cupcake or muffin wells & bake these at 350F- about 25 to 30 mins or till a toothpick inserted into the centers comes out clean of any wet batter. (Makes 2 dozen). They freeze well, too!

POPPYSEED LEMON MUFFINS

HAVE A MUFFIN — **The Perfect Muffin**

Jacobsen's makes a delightful assortment of muffins, offered at their Saginaw, Michigan store dining room. This is my favorite!

9-oz box yellow cake mix
¼-cup cold water
Dash nutmeg
1 tsp lemon extract
1 egg
1 TB sour cream
1 TB poppyseed
Butter & Sugar for Tops

Dump dry cake mix into 1½-qt mixing bowl. Stir in water & nutmeg & extract plus egg & sour cream, using fork to stir till you have a smooth dough. Combine well. Make sure that every single dry particle of the cake mix has been completely dissolved. (Electric mixer on low speed may also be used, but I caution you not to overbeat or muffins will turn out heavy!) Divide batter equally between 10 paper lined muffins wells or between 12 paper lined cupcake wells & bake at 400F-about 16 mins or till toothpick inserted into centers comes out clean. Cool in pan on rack 30 mins. Papers will stick to the muffin if peeled off too soon. (They freeze well, too!)

OLGA INSPIRED BREAD (Pita)

1 cup milk	1 tsp salt	1 tsp sugar
1/4-cup honey	1 pkg dry yeast	4 cups flour
1/4-cup margarine	1/4-cup warm water	1 large egg

Scald milk & remove to large bowl. Add honey, margarine & salt to the milk, stirring till margarine melts. Set aside. Allow it to cool to lukewarm. In a small bowl or cup sprinkle the yeast over the water & stir in sugar. Let stand 5 mins. Add 1½-cups of the flour to the lukewarm milk/honey mixture, beating till smooth with electric mixer. Beat in yeast mixture & egg. Add remaining 2½-cups flour little at a time, till you have a sticky dough. Dip kneading hand into just enough MORE flour that you can knead dough right in bowl till no longer sticky, and dough becomes smooth & elastic with small bubbles bursting just below the surface. Knead 2 mins. Place dough in greased large bowl, turning dough once to grease surface. Cover with another bowl same size, inverted & greased inside, too. Let dough rise 90 mins or till doubled. Punch down. Divide into 16 equal pieces. Roll each piece out to a 7 or 8" circle only 1/8" thick! Heat a large dry skillet over med-high (no grease on it) & bake each circle only 15-20 SECONDS, flipping to brown other side 10 seconds or till small brown spots appear. Don't overbake. Bread must be flexible. Remove with spatula to cool. Store in plastic food bags, continuing to roll & bake till all dough is used. Seal bags to retain moisture & either use, or refrigerate or freeze at once. Bread can be reheated on cookie sheets in 450F-oven 6 to 8 mins. makes 16.

SLOT-KEY'S TEXAS ROLLS

Imitate Schlotzsky'S ROLLS by mixing together in cup ½-cup warm water, 1 TB sugar, 1 pkg dry yeast. Let stand till it bubbles. In bowl mix together 3/4-cup warm milk, ½-tsp salt & 1/4-tsp baking soda dissolved in ½-TB water + 1 cup flour, till smooth. Beat in yeast mixture & 1½-cups more flour to make a thick sticky dough. Divide dough between 5 greased-and-dusted in cornmeal tins from Dinty Moore's 1½-lb Stew-to make perfect roll shapes. Cover each tin in square of greased waxed paper. Let rise 1 hr or till doubled. Remove squares of paper & spray tops of dough in Pam. Bake 375F-20 mins or till browned. Cool in tins. Slice & grill cut sides of rolls on buttered griddle. Fill as you wish.

Gloria Pitzer's MAKE ALIKE RECIPES — 15

BISCUITS
Inspired by both Popeye's & Hardee's — *Incredible*

1 cup Bisquick
1 TB sour cream
¼-cup Club Soda
½-tsp sugar

Mix all 4 ingredients together well in 1½-qt mixing bowl til smooth. Dip hand into just enough MORE Bisquick that you'll knead dough right in bowl till elastic, like bread dough. Now shape into 4 patties each 1" thick, placing close together in greased baking pan. Bake 450F- 18-20 mins or till gold-brown & doubled in size. Cool in pan on rack 10 mins before served. Makes 4 large biscuits. Recipe can be doubled!

Baking Powder Biscuits

Mix 2 c flour, 1 TB baking powder & 1 TB sugar, ½-tsp salt with 1/3 cup Crisco (not margarine, please), till crumbly. Make well in center & add 1/8-tsp baking soda dissolved 1st in 3/4-cup buttermilk. Pour into well. Mix thoroughly & then knead in bowl till smooth & eleastic, dipping hand into just enough more flour that dough doesn't stick to hand. Pat out 1" thick & cut into 3" rounds (using juice concentrate can as cutter), baking on greased baking pan, 450F-15-18 mins or till golden & doubled. Makes 8-10 biscuits.

PINEAPPLE CAKE (Mama's Make-It-In-A-Minute Cake)
From Carole Arnold, talk-show MC at KTOK-Radio, Okla City, OK

KTOK CAKE

1-lb can crushed pineapple canned in its own juice
2 eggs
2 tsp baking SODA
2 cups sugar
2 cups flour
Ready-to-use Sour Cream Icing

PINEAPPLE CAKE

Dump pineapple, juice & all, into med bowl. Beat in each remaining ingredient just as listed, beating med-speed of mixer ½-min with each addition. Pour batter into greased 9x13" pan, & bake at 350F- almost 40 mins or till toothpick inserted in center comes out clean. Cool in pan on rack & apply icing. Serves 8 to 10 nicely. (A very moist, light cake.

Gloria Pitzer's MAKE ALIKE RECIPES

Fantastic Loaves

SO GOOD — You'll like it better...

FRANKENMUTH FRUIT STOLLEN

¼-cup warm water
1 TB sugar
2 pkgs dry yeast
1 tsp vanilla
1½-cups canned Borden's Eggnog
3½-cups all-purpose flour
¼-tsp cinnamon
2 cups mixed, diced candied fruits

Place warm water in measuring cup. Stir in sugar and yeast. Let stand 5 minutes or till bubbly. Stir in the vanilla and pour mixture into 2½-quart mixing bowl. With electric mixer on medium, beat in the eggnog and about half of the flour till you have the consistency of a cake batter. Remove beaters. Work in remaining flour till you have soft dough, and all flour has dissolved. Dip hands into additional flour to knead the dough in the bowl till smooth and elastic, working in the fruits as you knead the dough. Place dough in smooth ball in large greased mixing bowl. Invert another bowl, same diameter, also greased inside, over the bowl of dough. Let rise till doubled —(about 90 mins) in a warm place. Punch down dough and knead it again till smooth, shaping it into a round loaf that will fit a greased and floured 10" Pyrex pie plate. Find a cake carrier cover, or a large enough bowl that it will fit over the loaf without the bread touching it as it rises in a warm place till doubled. Place in a COLD OVEN and at once set temperature at 425F—for only 8 minutes. At once then reduce temperature to 350F—for 30 mins —or till crust appears nicely browned and it makes a hollow sound when you tap it with your fingers. Cool in pie plate on wire rack about an hour. Do not attempt to cut the bread for at least 4 hours. Makes one round loaf.

TO SLICE THE ROUND LOAF - First cut the loaf in half from top to bottom and then each half in half again so that you have 4 wedges. Now slice each wedge into 1" thick slices, also from top to bottom to give you half slices of bread.

Simple

TOO MUCH FLOUR on your hands, when you knead your yeast dough, will make it dry and crumbly—not soft and moist. Keep the amount of flour to an absolute minimum —sufficient enough that the dough is no longer sticky and feels very elastic. Then knead it for all you're worth — right in the bowl. The more you knead it the better it will be!

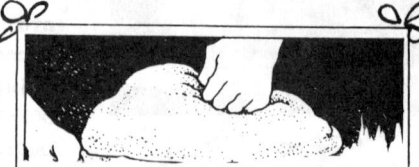

KNEADING When a recipe gives a range of flour instead of a specific amount, start with the smallest amount given & add as much as necessary just to make dough no longer sticky & quite elastic in texture. Less flour means lighter bread. As soon as dough feels smooth & elastic, it's ready to rise in a warm place till doubled. The more you punch it down & let it rise, the lighter, too, it will be when it is baked.

GLORIA PITZER'S MAKE ALIKE RECIPES 17

Escalloped Apples Inspired by frozen food's

Mix together 3-lb peeled, cored, diced apples, 4-serving-size box lemon Jell-O powder, 1/3 cup Bisquick, 1 TB apple pie spice, ¼-cup water. Spoon evenly into greased 9" baking dish (square or round) & bake uncovered at 350F- 35-40 mins or till apples are tender to the bite. Serve as sidedish or dessert.

(*) COOKIE SHEET

(*)COOKIE-BAKING SHEET PREPARATION: Spray cookie sheet in Pam & place in 375F—oven, empty, 3 to 4 mins or till Pam turns brown. Wipe off brown Pam with paper towel, leaving light but even film. Drop cookies at once onto warm cookie sheet, baking per recipe directions. DO NOT REGREASE between batches of cookies. This process is good for baking 7 dozen cookies before it must be regreased.

Homestyle — comes close

MARY ANN STYLE
OLD-FASHIONED
FROSTED SPICE COOKIES
3 eggs
1 cup dark raisins
1 tsp baking soda
2 tsp apple pie spice
1 TB cinnamon
1 TB paprika
1 tsp vanilla

Put all ingredients as listed into blender. Blend on/off speed, high, about 1 minute or till raisins are so finely ground that these resemble coarse pepper. Set mixture aside. Get out your large mixing bowl, line up the following ingredients:

½-lb (2 sticks) margarine
1 cup granulated sugar
1 cup packed DARK brown sugar
"The Blender Mixture"
2 cups self-rising flour
1½-cups Quaker quick oats —used dry

On high speed with electric mixer, cream margarine till smooth, beating in both sugars till light & fluffy. Beat in "The Blender Mixture" & then the flour a little at a time till it disappears. Work in rolled oats. Prepare cookie sheet (*). Use a plastic Rubbermain ice cream scoop in which to measure dough for each cookie, or measure dough by packing it into ¼-cup measuring cup, minus 1 TB. Shape each portion pf the dough into oblong form about 2" by 4", placing these 2" apart on (*)prepared cookie sheet. Bake at 350F—exactly 12 minutes. Let cookies cool on baking sheet 5 mins. Remove carefully to complete cooling on paper towels. Makes about 3 dozen cookies. (*) See Index for Cookie sheet preparation

FROSTING—Open a 1-lb container of ready-to-spread vanilla icing. Place it in top of double boiler, over gently simmering water & stir frosting till warm and melted. Stir in 1 tsp anise extract (a licroice flavored extract). Apply this warm icing to cookies soon as you remove them from the oven and before you remove them from the cookie sheets.

FRUIT SNACK APPLETTES

2 TB unflavored gelatin
½-cup cold apple juice
2 cups sugar
¾-cup apple juice
1 cup chopped walnuts
1 tsp vanilla

Soak gelatin in the ½-cup cold apple juice. Put the sugar with remaining apple juice into 2½-qt saucepan, stirring constantly over medium high heat, until it comes to a boil. Turn heat to gentle simmer. Stir in softened gelatin mixture. Stir to blend and simmer quite gently, while continuing to stir, for 5 minutes. Remove from heat. Let stand till it begins to thicken. Stir in walnuts & vanilla. Pour into lightly oiled 8" square pan. Chill till firm. Cut into squares. Dust squares lightly in sifted powdered sugar. Makes about 3 dozen pieces.

Gloria Pitzer's MAKE ALIKE RECIPES

Doing it right

OVEN PANCAKE Inspired by House of Pancake

3 eggs
1/2-cup milk
1/2-cup flour
dash salt

3 TB oil*
(see note below)

Serves 2 nicely

For Apple Pancake:
   1 large peeled, cored thinly
     sliced cooking apple
   Lemon Juice & Powdered Sugar

For Garden Griddlecake:
   HALF of 10-oz pkg frozen chopped
     broccoli, cooked & drained
   HALF of 10-oz pkg frozen mixed
     vegetables, cooked & drained
   1 cup shredded Swiss cheese

Place 1st **4 ingredients** into blender. Blend high speed 1 min or till smooth. Put oil into oven-proof 10" skillet & pour blender batter into oil so that batter "floats"* on the oil. If not enough oil is used pancake will stick to pan later. For Apple Pancake sprinkle apple slices evenly over batter to within 1" of edge. For Garden Style spoon broccoli & vegetables evenly over batter. Either way, bake at 400F- about 20 mins or till "set" & golden brown with sides of pancake having curled up over rim of pan like a pale yellow bowl. Remove at once to serving platter. For Garden variety quickly sprinkle top with cheese & place it a few inches from broiler heat just to melt cheese. Sprinkle apple variety in lemon juice & powdered sugar.

It's a 'secret'!

CHOCOLATE MOUSSE PIE Inspired by The Olive Garden's

Soften 1 envelope unflavored gelatine powder in ¼-cup cold water till mushry. Set in heatproof cup in pan hot water till clear. Combine with 6 cups (1 serving size each) Jell-O brand ready to serve chocolate pudding & 3 cups thawed Cool Whip (8-oz tub). Spread in 9" baked & cooled pie shell or crumb crust, piling filling artistically into shell. Refrigerate it 24 hrs before serving. Garnish servings in additional Cool Whip & shaved Hershey bar. Serves 6 to 8 adequately OR 2 with no sense of conscience!

Gloria Pitzer's MAKE ALIKE RECIPES

STRAWBERRY LEATHER (Candy)

In blender combine 1-qt strawberries, washed & hulled with ¼-cup honey using on/off speed till smooth. Line cookie sheet or dehydrator tray with Seran Wrap & pour mixture onto tray ½" thick. Bake in vented oven (door ajar) at 150F- 15 hrs or place in dehydrator at 140F- about 3 days. When dry tightly wrap in Seran. Drying time depends on moisture content of food. If using dehydrator be sure to rotate trays every 12 hours. If using oven turn strawberry mixture after 10 hours so leather is not sticky.

DESSERT

CHOCOLATE GRAVY (Topping for desserts)

An old-fashioned recipe with contemporary possibilities.

Into your blender put: 2 cups milk, 3/4-cup sugar, 2 TB unsweetened dry cocoa, 2 TB flour, ½-tsp salt. Blend on high speed till smooth. Pour into saucepan & cook, stirring constantly on med-high, just as you would to make a pudding, continuing until it becomes smooth & thickened. It should be the consistency of gravy. Remove then from heat & stir in 2 TB butter or margarine & 1 tsp vanilla. Serve it spooned over hot, split buttered biscuits as a dessert, or over sliced poundcake or plain cake. Makes about 2 cups gravy. (It also goes nicely over ice cream as a warm topping!)

Fudge Topping

BREAD without yeast

1 cup buttermilk
1/3 cup corn oil
1½-tsp vanilla
2 eggs

2 cups all purpose flour
1 cup granulated sugar
4 tsp baking powder
1 tsp salt

Inspired by Sanders - Michigan (1950's) BATTER BREAD

Preheat your oven to 350F— and grease and flour (or spray in Pam or Baker's Joy) a 9x5" bread loaf pan. In an accomodating bowl, combine the ingredients just as I have listed them and beat with an electric mixer at medium high speed for about 4 minutes. Pour batter into prepared pan and bake at 350F—about 50 minutes or till toothpick inserted in center comes out clean. The bread will develop a deep crack down the middle of the top as it bakes and eventhough it appears to be browning well, you have to be sure it is thoroughly baked inside or it will fall-kerplopp! So the best test to see if it is done is to insert a paper-covered, wire trash bag twist through the center. Be certain it touches the bottom of the pan when you insert it. If it comes out clean of any wet batter, it is done! Remove from oven and at once remove it from the pan. Let it cool completely on a wire rack before slicing it to serve. Makes 1 loaf.

Gloria Pitzer's MAKE ALIKE RECIPES

PETTIT FOURS PARTY CAKES — Innovative

Prepare & bake white or yellow 18-oz cake mix per box directions. Bake in two 9x13x2" pan (producing thin layers) per box directions, reducing baking time 20% or till toothpick inserted into center of cakes comes out clean. Bake only one pan at a time. When completely cooled (on wire racks), cut into 3x3" squares. Place on waxed paper lined cookie sheets. Freeze 1 hour uncovered or till solid. Meanwhile empty 1-lb container ready-to-spready vanilla frosting into top of double boiler over gently simmering water stirring till thinned & warm. But do not dilute! With tip of sharp knife, pierce frozen pieces of cake, one at a time, dipping to coat in warm frosting, letting excess drip back into pan. Air dry & decorate with tubes of ready-to-use frosting with decorator's tips or apply candy rosettes from Betty Crocker to top of each piece frosted cake, using dab of frosting to secure flowers in place. Makes 48 pieces.

ELEPHANT EARS
Inspired by Farmer's Market's L.A. STYLE

Beat 5 egg yolks till thick, adding 3 TB sugar little at a time, beating with mixer on med-speed. Add 1-tsp grated lemon rind, 1½-tsp almond extract, 5 TB sour cream, beating 2 mins. Remove beaters. Work in ¼-tsp salt, 2½-cups all-purpose flour. Knead in bowl till dough is pliable. Cover bowl & let stand 1 hour. Roll out a third of dough at a time on lightly floured surface. Keep it thin-less than ¼". Cut in 5" circles using saucer as guide & drop 1 at time into 400 degree hot oil 2" deep. Fry each side few mins or till nice golden color. Dust in powdered sugar while warm. Makes many.

CHOCOLATE CUPCAKES Inspired by Sanders

A nice old-fashioned chocolate cupcake recipe you can make from scratch — like Grandma used to — or should have!

¼-cup vegetable or corn oil
¾-cup granulated sugar
1 large egg
1 tsp vanilla
¼-tsp salt
1 tsp baking soda
2/3 cup milk
2 TB lemon juice
1/3 cup unsweetened dry cocoa
1 cup all-purpose flour

In 2-qt mixing bowl, with electric mixer on med-speed, beat oil, sugar & egg till smooth. Beat in vanilla, salt & soda, beating 2 mins. Put milk & lemon juice into cup & then pour into batter, beating 1 minute. Beat in cocoa powder & flour, scraping down sides & bottom of bowl often. Beat 3 mins. Divide batter equally between 12 paper lined cupcake wells & bake at 350F—25 mins or till toothpick inserted into centers comes out clean. Cool in pan 15 mins. Frost as desired. (Makes 1 dozen).

Gloria Pitzer's MAKE ALIKE RECIPES

CHOCOLATE CHUNK PECAN COOKIES
Inspired by Nabisco's Chips Ahoy Selections!

- 2 eggs
- 2 tsp vanilla
- 1 cup sugar
- 6 TB Crisco (solid not oil)
- 3 cups Bisquick
- 12-oz milk chocolate morsels
- 1½-cups broken pecans

In medium bowl using electric mixer medium speed, beat eggs & vanilla till foamy. Beat in sugar, little at time till smooth. Beat in Crisco till creamy. Remove beaters. Work in Bisquick with spoon. Finally get your hands into dough & work it smooth. Work in morsels & pecans. Shape dough into long roll about 2½" in diameter. Wrap in double sheets waxed paper, twisting ends tightly. Refrigerate 1 hour. Slice rolls of dough ¼" thick, placing 2" apart on ungreased baking sheets. Bake at 375F— only 12 mins or till "set" & delicately browned. Cool 5 mins on baking sheets before removing carefully to paper towels to continue cooling. Makes 5 dozen cookies

REMARKABLE

CHIPS IN THE MIDDLE COOKIES Prove It To Yourself
Inspired by Sunshine's product

Prepare the cookies exactly as directed in recipe above but omit the pecans and use SEMI-SWEET morsels instead. Assemble baked & cooled cookies flat sides together, sandwich style, with the following filling:

Open a 1-lb can chocolate frosting & empty into top of double boiler, over gently simmering water. soften 1-envelope Knox unflavored gelatine powder in ¼-cup cold water till mushy, in heat-proof cup. Then set cup inside pan hot water till gelatine becomes transparent (few minutes). Vigorously stir it into frosting. Heat mixture only till lukewarm. Transfer to 1½-qt mixing bowl, using electric mixer, high speed, beating in 4 TB solid Crisco, beating till smooth. Apply icing between 2 baked & cooled cookies, bottom sides, sandwich style. Enough to fill 2½-dozen sandwich cookies.

OUR FAVORITE

BAKED PECAN HALVES TO SNACK ON

Coat 12-oz pecan halves in 4 or 5 TB bottled liquid margarine & spread evenly in bottom of greased baking pan. Bake at 350F— about 12-15 mins, stirring once or twice during baking time. Remove from pan at once when pecans are golden brown. Watch them! They scorch easily! Spread immediately over paper towels to cool. Store in covered-container at room temperature.

Gloria Pitzer's MAKE ALIKE RECIPES

NEW CONCEPT
APPLE STRUEDEL
(Inspired by Dawn Donuts)

Simple

- 2 rolls (8-oz each) Crescent Dinner Rolls
- 20-oz can apple pie filling
- ½-cup chopped walnuts
- ½-cup raisins
- ¼-cup flour
- ¼-cup melted butter
- 1 tsp cinnamon
- ¼-cup packed light brown sugar
- 1-lb container ready-to-spread vanilla icing

Spray jelly roll pan (13½x9½x1") in Pam. Unroll 1 roll of Crescent Dinner Rolls to cover pan. Mix all of remaining ingredients EXCEPT icing, in mixing bowl. Spread to within ½" of edge of dough. Unroll 2nd tube of Crescent Dinner Roll dough & place over top. Pinch 4 seams to seal in filling. Wipe surface of dough in either melted butter or sour cream, smearing lightly but evenly. Bake at 400F- 15 to 18 mins or till golden brown. Meanwhile Micro warm the ready-to-use icing (frosting) in bowl OR heat it in top of double boiler over simmering water till warmed & thinned. Drizzle over top of struedel soon as you remove it from oven. Let cool on wire rack 30 mins. Ciut into diagonal bars. Serves 6 nicely or 2 teenagers.

cheesecake
New York-style
Inspired by Cathy's Cheesecakes of Michigan, as served at the Buggyworks Restaurant 1991

Generously grease the insides of a 9" springform pan in margarine or spray with Pam. Mix 1½-cups fine Graham cracker crumbs with 1 envelope unflavored gelatine & ¼-cup sugar. Dust the inside of greased pan in crumb mixture. Shake out excess onto plate & reserve, refrigerate to use again some other time. Set pan aside. Prepare the filling. In large mixing bowl, using electric mixer med-speed, combine 3 pkgs (8-oz ea) cream cheese at room temperature with 8-oz sour cream, 2 TB butter, 2 TB cornstarch, 2 lg eggs, 1¼-cups of sugar, 1 tsp vanilla. Beat 3 mins to blend well. Pour into prepared pan. Bake at 350F- 50 mins or till knife inserted 1" from edge of pan (not center) comes out clean. Center is continuing to bake in its own heat while cooling. Cool 1 hr on wire rack. Then refrigerate 4 hours before removing from pan to cut & serve. Serves 10-12. Keep it refrigerated.

WHITE CAKE MIX (Homemade)

2 cups flour
1½ cups granulated sugar
4 tsp baking powder
1 tsp salt
¼-lb margarine cut into bits
3 TB oil

Put everything listed into large bowl, using low speed of an electric mixer blending till the consistency of fine gravel. Keep refrigerated in covered container to be used within 3 months. Do not double this recipe. But you can cut it in half, which makes a single 9" layer, equal to a 9-oz of Jiffy Cake Mix. The above recipe is equal to an 18-oz box cake mix (two 9" layers).

To Use This Cake Mix:

5 cups (all of above mix)
1 cup milk
1½ tsp vanilla
5 egg whites

Beat all 4 ingredients on med-speed of electric mixer for 5 to 6 mins, rotating bowl in direction the opposite of which beaters are turning. Scrape down sides & bottom of bowl often. Do NOT underbeat. Divide then between 2 greased & floured 9" layer pans, also lined in sheet waxed paper, top side greased also. Bake at 350F— 35 to 40 mins or till tester inserted into center comes out clean. Cool in pans on rack 30 mins. Remove to plate & assemble with frosting.

SPICE CAKE MIX
Inspired by Duncan Hines

To make your own Spice Cake Mix out of an 18-oz box white or yellow cake mix (or recipe above), simply stir into dry cake mix: 1 TB apple pie spice, 1 tsp bottled, grated orange peel & 1 tsp bottled lemon peel, plus ½-tsp nutmeg & ½-tsp cinnamon. Prepare as box (or recipe above) otherwise directs.

FROSTING MIX — Coconut-Pecan Flavor
Inspired by Coconut-Pecan Frosting Mix from Pillsbury

COCONUT-PECAN FROSTING MIX called for in many Pillsbury Bake Off recipes, can be made with this mix. Combine 1 box dry vanilla frosting mix with 1 box dry chocolate frosting mix. Add 1 cup chopped pecans, 1 cup oven-toasted-till-golden flaked coconut, cooled. Divide mixture in half. Half of this mixture will equal 1 box of the Pillsbury Coconut Pecan Frosting Mix of years ago. Half of mix can then be prepared per box directions as given on either the vanilla or chocolate frosting mix.

HOMEMADE MIXES

Caramel Icing — Homestyle

In medium saucepan, over med-heat, stir together ½-cup butter & 1 cup packed light brown sugar, till butter melts & sugar dissolves. Stir in ¼-cup milk & stirring constantly, bring just to a boil. Boil 1 minute while stirring. Remove from heat. Use electric mixer to beat in 2 cups powdered sugar & ¼-tsp vanilla. Beat till thick enough to spread. Fills & frosts a double 9" layer cake.

In pursuit of challenge

This Amish favorite is a sandwich cookie or cake that is filled with a smooth, creamy frosting – a blue ribbon winner at county fairs in Pennsylvania Dutch country!

WHOOPIE PIES (Or Devil Dogs)

- 6 tablespoons shortening
- 1 cup sugar
- 1 egg
- 2 cups flour
- ½ cup cocoa
- ¼ teaspoon salt
- ½ cup buttermilk
- 1 teaspoon vanilla
- 1 teaspoon baking soda
- ½ cup hot water

In each of the Amish cookbooks that I consulted on this recipe, I found the ingredients the same, but the measurements varied somewhat. The Amish version of this wonderful dessert is a trustworthy recipe to add to your files!

Cream shortening until light; add sugar gradually, continuing to cream all the while. Beat in egg. Sift flour, cocoa and salt. Combine buttermilk and vanilla. Add sifted dry ingredients to creamed mixture alternately with buttermilk/vanilla combination. Dissolve soda in water and beat into flour mixture. (Mixture will be more the consistency of a thick cake batter than a cookie dough.) Drop by rounded teaspoonfuls onto well-greased cookie sheets, spacing about 1½ inches apart, and making cookies as uniform as possible. Bake at 400 degrees 8 to 10 minutes or until a finger pressed in center of cookie leaves a print that springs back slowly. Remove to wire racks to cool.

CREAM FILLING

- ¾ cup shortening
- 2½ to 3 cups sifted powdered sugar
- 1 egg white
- 1 teaspoon vanilla

Beat shortening and 1 cup sugar until fluffy; beat in egg white and vanilla. Beat in enough of remaining sugar to make a frosting of good spreading consistency.

When cookies are cool, sandwich together with a thick layer of filling. Makes about 2 dozen cream-filled cookies.

Gloria Pitzer's MAKE ALIKE RECIPES

IMITATED A REMEMBRANCE
GIRL SCOOT MINT COOKIES
INSPIRED MINT COOKIE (1985)

CHOCOLATE MINT COOKIES
Inspired by the Girl Scout's

18-oz box devil's food cake mix
2 small boxes instant chocolate pudding powder
1 cup Bisquick
2 cups MIRACLE WHIP
2 tsp mint extract

In large mixing bowl with mixer on high speed, combine 1st 3 dry ingredients till thoroughly mixed. Dump in Miracle Whip & extract & beat on high speed till dough becomes smooth & leaves sides of the bowl nicely. You'll note this is <u>the only liquid the recipe needs!</u> Let dough stand 10 mins before using to air-dry it a bit. Cookies shape better that way. To measure cookie dough, use <u>measuring teaspoon</u> firmly packed & leveled off over rim of bowl. Place 2" apart on cookie sheet lightly sprayed in Pam & then lightly wiped off with napkin to remove excess Pam. Bake exactly 8 mins at 350F-. Do NOT overbake. Immediately upon removing cookies from oven gently flatten each cookie with back of spatula with no holes in it. Cool on baking sheets 5 mins. Then dip each cookie, one at a time, in the prepared warm chocolate coating from the following recipe:

CHOCOLATE COATING FOR COOKIES

1/4 of a bar of Gulf canning paraffin, grated on large hole
    of vegetable grater so it will melt more quickly
2 pkgs (12-oz ea) semi-sweet chocolate morsels
2 tsp mint extract

Be patient in melting the above combined ingredients over HOT---not boiling water, stirring often with fork till smooth & warm. Keep it warm over hot water while you coat the cookies, coating only about HALF of each cookie which makes it easier to do than trying to coat the entire cookie. Let cookies dry on greassed waxed paper lined cookie sheets till set. Then store in covered container in refrigerator.

Gloria Pitzer's MAKE ALIKE RECIPES

CHOCOLATE CHUNK COOKIES
Inspired by J. L. Hudson's of 1950's & 60's downtown Detroit

½-lb butter or margarine
1 cup packed brown sugar
1 cup granulated sugar
3 medium eggs (2 large)
1½-tsp vanilla
1 tsp baking soda

3 cups self-rising flour
4-oz pecans chopped or broken
8-oz (2 bars) German Sweet
 Chocolate hammered into
 pea-sized pieces

Only the name remains the same

In mixing bowl with electric mixer high speed, cream butter, 3 mins. Beat in each remaining ingredient, EXCEPT pecans and chocolate, beating ½-minute after each addition. Remove beaters & work in pecans & chocolate. Measure 2 TB dough for each cookie, shaping into mounds & pacing 2" apart on cookie sheet lightly sprayed in Pam. Bake at 350F- 14 mins or till there are little bits of wet dough in small cracked spots on tops of cookies. DO NOT OVERBAKE. Cookies continue to bake in their own heat while cooling 5 mins on cookie sheets on wire rack. Remove carefully to continue cooling on paper towels. 2½-doz. (Cookies will be very hard later if overbaked!)

OATMEAL RAISIN COOKIES J.L. Hudson Style
Inspired by the wonderful soft-cookies-that-stayed-soft from the counters at the Farmer Street entrance of the downtown Detroit store in the 1950's. To the following basic Oatmeal Cookie recipe, you can add 1 cup raisins & 1 cup chopped walnuts & continue as the recipe otherwise directs, except that it will make 1½-dozen more.

SOFT OATMEAL COOKIES THAT STAY SOFT!
Inspired by J. L. Hudson Downtown Detroit 1950

UNIQUE

¼-cup melted butter
¼-cup sour cream
1 tsp vanilla
1 tsp cinnamon

2/3 cup sugar
1 large egg
2 cups Bisquick not packed
1 cup quick-cooking rolled oats

Reverse the order in which ingredients are put together using 1st ingredient last, etc., & you get CRISPY cookies

Beat 1st 6 ingredients together with mixer, high speed till smooth. Beat in Bisquick & oats. Drop by rounded TBspoonful 2" apart on lightly greased baking sheets. Flatten each to ¼" thick round with cup bottom greased & dipped into sugar with each cookie flattened. Place raisin in center of each. Bake at 375F- 8-10 mins till barely brown around edges, but tops of cookies are still WHITE! Cool on baking sheets 5 min & remove carefully to paper towels. Do NOT overbake! Makes 2½-dozen.

Gloria Pitzer's MAKE ALIKE RECIPES

THE BEST!
LEMON BLENDER ICING

1 tsp lemon extract
2 TB light Karo Syrup
4 TB margarine - softened
Dash Nutmeg

Dash of Salt
1/3 cup buttermilk
1 TB grated lemon peel
2 cups powdered sugar

As listed put all ingredients into blender, blending high speed half a minute or till smooth. Refrigerate unused icing, covered, to use within a 2 week period. Freeze to use within a year. Makes 1½-cups.

DESSERTS

SUGAR FREE

SUGAR-FREE CHEESECAKE

Coat a greased 9" square baking dish in very fine potato chip crumbs (salted or salt-free). Shake out excess crumbs. Beat 2 pkgs (8-oz each) cream cheese with 4-TB sour cream till smooth, using electric mixer high speed. Set aside. Dissolve a 4-serving size pkg Sugar-Free Jell-O (lemon or pineapple or other flavor) in 1 cup boiling water. Refrigerate till completely cooled. Gradually beat into cream cheese mixture. Set aside. Prepare a 4-serving size pkg sugar-free instant vanilla pudding with only 1½-cup milk (2% is fine). The pkg tells you to use 2 cups but you only need 1½-for this recipe. When smooth, beat pudding mixture into cream cheese mixture. Pour into prepared pan. Refrigerate 24 hours, covered in plastic wrap. Garnish each serving in finely chopped walnuts or pecans or fresh fruit. Serves 9

DESSERT PIZZA —— Dessert Pizza
Inspired by Godfather's

Thaw 1 loaf of frozen bread dough until you can knead it in a greased bowl with slightly greased fingers. Shape it then to fit a Pam-sprayed 12" pizza pan. Brush surface ligthly but evenly with bottled liquid margarine or melted butter. Dust then evenly but lightly in a mixture of 2 TB sugar & 1 tsp cinnamon. Prepare a streussel topping by combining in a small bowl: 1/3 cup packed light brown sugar, 1/3 cup all-purpose flour, 4 TB bottled liquid margarine or melted butter, 1 tsp vanilla. When crumbly sprinkle evenly over surface of dough. Let rise 15 mins in a warm place while you preheat oven to 450F. Bake the dessert pizza at 450F-about 20-to-25 mins or till golden brown. Immediately out of oven, place on rack to cool a few minutes & drizzle with half of a 1-lb container of ready-to-spread vanilla frosting that you have warmed in the top of a double boiler over gently simmering water, till "pourable". Cut like a pizza & serve at once. Serves several sensibly or 1 teenager.

Gloria Pitzer's MAKE ALIKE RECIPES

CREAM FILLING RECIPES
FILLING FOR DONUTS

2 cups strawberry soda pop (Faygo brand preferred)
1 cup strawberry jelly (not jam)
¼-cup cornstarch

NO FAT

Put all 3 ingredients through blender, high speed, half a minute or till smooth. Pour into small saucepan & cook, stirring constantly with wire whisk, over med-high heat till thickened & smooth. This takes about 5 mins. Remove from heat. Cool to lukewarm. Funnel filling into a plastic ketchup dispenser with the pointed-tip cap. When filling donuts, insert that pointed tip into side of fried, still warm donut & squeeze to emit required filling per recipe. (3 TB for large donuts & 1 TB for biscuit size donuts).

CREAM PUFF & DONUT FILLING

Soften 1 envelope unflavored gelatine in ¼-cup cold water few minutes till mushy. In a heat-proof cup, set in pan of hot water (or Microwave on "warm") till mixture is clear. Beat this mixture into 17-oz canned ready-to-use Thank You Brand vanilla pudding. Fills a dozen cream puffs or large donuts. Keep refrigerated.

PASTRY HORNS CREAM FILLING

24 large marshmallows	6-serving size (large) box
½-cup milk	**Cook-N-Serve** vanilla pudding
1-lb butter or margarine	2 envelopes unflavored gelatine
1½-cups powdered sugar	1/3 cup cold water

In medium saucepan, melt marshmallows in milk, stirring low heat till smooth. Refrigerate mixture, covered, till completely cold. Beat mixture in medium bowl with electric mixer till light, adding butter (or margarine) little at a time till smooth. Gradually beat in powdered sugar till creamy. Refrigerate while you prepare the pudding per box directions. When you remove pudding from heat, set aside & soften gelatine in cold water till mushy. Beat mushy gelatine mixture into hot pudding. Let cool & refrigerate till very cold. Beat pudding mixture into frosting marshmallow mixture. Fills 2 dozen horns or cream puffs. Recipe may be cut in half to fill 1 dozen pastries. Keep refrigerated.

CREAM FILLING FOR ECLAIRS & CANOLLI

Into blender put 3 cups milk, a 6-serving size box **Cook-N-Serve** vanilla pudding powder & 2 raw egg yolks. Blend high speed half a minute or till smooth. Transfer to medium saucepan, stirring constantly with wire whisk on med-high heat about 5 mins or till thickened & smooth. Remove at once from heat & pour carefully into another pan or bowl without disturbing the bottom of pan where it is possible some of the pudding has overcooked & scorched a little. Let stand while you soften 1 envelope Knox unflavored gelatine powder in ¼-cup cold water till mushy – few minutes. Whisk this into hot pudding till dissolved. Cool completely before using.

Gloria Pitzer's MAKE ALIKE RECIPES

PACZKI (Pronounced "Punch Keys")

The Polish custom of having these wonderful rich, filled, glazed donuts on the day before Lent begins has spilled over into every other ethnic group since Paczkis were first introduced to Americans. In Hamtramck, Michigan, the largest Polish population outside of the country of Poland, orders for these donuts are taken for weeks before the day-before-Lent begins. On a normal day the Oaza Bakery would produce about 120 dozen. Tradition for some dictates eating them, for others it dictates making them! I have 2 versions - the authentic & my own American shortcut - the Gringo version!

authentic

The Authentic Recipe for Paczki: (Recipe may be cut in half!)

3 cups milk
½-lb butter-softened
1 tsp salt
3/4-cup sugar
12 egg yolks
2 tsp vanilla

2 packets dry yeast
1 tsp sugar
¼-cup warm water
12-cups all-purpose flour
4½-lbs solid shortening for frying
or 3 pints vegetable oil

(This recipe makes 40 donuts.)

Scald milk. Cool to room temperature in large mixing bowl. Add the butter, salt, sugar. Beat in egg yolks & vanilla. Dissolve yeast with sugar in the warm water, stirring once or twice. Let stand few minutes till bubbly. Add to milk mixture. Begin adding flour, 1 cup at a time, stirring till dough becomes too thick to manage with mixing spoon. Begin using your hands to work the dough to smooth eleastic, non-sticky texture. When doiugh begins to come away from the sides of the bowl, stop adding flour & knead briefly. Transfer dough to large greased bowl. Cover with inverted bowl same size, also greased inside. Let dough rise till doubled in volume. Punch down. Let rise again (about 90 mins) in warm place. Punch down & shape into balls each about size of a golf ball. Let rise on greased waxed paper, placing 3 to 4" apart. (Be sure to grease hands when shaping into balls.) Let balls rise till doubled. Drop puffy balls, few at a time into 385F-hot oil or melted solid Crisco & fry few mins each side till golden brown. Turn with tongs. Don't be disappointed if donuts collapse when dropped into oil. This is normal. Won't hurt them at all. Gently remove from oil with tongs when browned. Let cool on rack to drain few mins. Using a plastic ketcup dispenser with pointed tip cap, filled with jelly or your own filling, insert pointed tip into side of donut & squeeze to allow about 3 TB filling into donut. Dust in powdered sugar or glaze with thin icing. **Makes 40 donuts.**

GRINGO PUNCH-KEY DONUT RECIPE Paczki PDQ

Unwrap & separate 10 biscuits from a tube of ready-to-bake biscuit dough (like Pillsbury's or Hungry Jack). In an electric skillet in 2 to 3" of oil at 385F fry these few at a time till golden brown, both sides, about 5 to 6 mins. Remove to rack to drain. MAKE A **FILLING** per recipe above & insert into donuts as described above.

Gloria Pitzer's MAKE ALIKE RECIPES

FUDGE CAKE Inspired by Shoney's/Big Boy

Prepare & bake a devil's food cake from an 18-oz box of cake mix, per box directions, using 9x13x2" pan. When completely cooled, cut cake into 3x3" squares, placing 2" thick slice of vanilla ice cream between 2 squares cake. Take with fudge sauce prepared this way:

FUDGE SAUCE - Melt 6-oz (1-cupful) semi-sweet morsels with 6 TB butter or margarine over low heat. Stir in 1-lb powdered sugar alternately with 12-oz can of Pet Milk, stirring constantly on low heat, till smooth & thickened. Add 1 tsp vanilla. Remove from heat. Beat just to blend well. Cool before spooning over cake & ice cream. Makes 4 to 6 servings———

RICE PUDDING Greek Style Without Raisins
Inspired by 4-Star Family Restaurant - Marysville, Mich.

We don't tell too many people about the 5-Star, only because we don't want to have to stand in a line any longer than we already do now when we go there 3 or 4 times a week for dinner. I have my favorites among which is their homemade rice pudding, which has the magic ingredient of Cream Of Wheat stirred into it as noted below, to thicken it and keep it creamy!

2 cups boiling water
1½-cups Minute Premium Rice
½-cup sugar
½-tsp salt
2/3 cup very hot milk
1 tsp vanilla
2 TB butter or margarine
1 packet Mix & Eat
    Cream of "Wheat (dry)

Combine 1st 4 ingredients. Boil hard 1 min. Stir well. Remove from heat. Cover; let stand 10 mins. Stir in milk & vanilla & butter. Sprinkle Cream of Wjheat over this, stirring well to dissolve quickly. Cover again. Let stand again 10 mins. Transfer to refrigerator container with tight-fitting lid. Refrigerate overnight or several hrs before serving icy cold, dusting each scoop in cinnamon if you wish & topping it off with Cool Whip. Freeze to use in 4 months. Serves 4 to 6.

Belgian Waffle   What a difference

Prepare your favorite waffle recipe from a boxed mix or a from-scratch recipe & to each cup of batter, beat in 1 TB bottled Carnation brand "original" malted milk powder - a product sold where ice cream toppings are found. Prepare per manufacturer's directions on waffle iron———

Gloria Pitzer's MAKE ALIKE RECIPES

PERFECT LEMON LAYER CAKE
Inspired by Sanders' 1950's

Create a Sensation

- 8-oz tub margarine
- 2 cups powdered sugar
- 1 TB lemon extract
- 3 large eggs
- 2 cups self-rising flour
- ½-cup sour cream
- 1 recipe lemon filling (Recipe below)

An American Favorite

Cream margarine with powdered sugar, with mixer on high speed, till light & fluffy (3 mins). Add extract. Beat 1 min. Add 1 egg, beating 1 min. measure out flour into bowl. Add a third of flour, beating 1 min. Add 1 more egg & half of remaining flour. Beat 1 min. Add last egg & last of flour, beating 1 min. Scrape bottom & sides of bowl often. Divide batter equally between 2 greased/floured 9" round layer pans. Crack each pan firmly on solid surface few times to break air bubbles & level batter. Bake at 325F- 40 mins or till tester inserted into centers comes out clean. Cool in pans on rack 20 mins. Assemble layers with filling applied between layers & over top. Garnish in chocolate sprinkles or chopped walnuts.

LEMON FILLING: Put 1 cup cold water, 4-serving size box lemon jell-O powder, ¼-cup cornstarch into blender. Blend high speed 1 min or till smooth. Pour into saucepan. Cook, stirring constantly with wire whisk, high heat, gradually adding 1½-cups boiling 7-UP or Squirt. Stir till comes to boil, is smooth & thickened. Remove from heat. Cool to lukewarm. Apply between layers & spread over top, allowing excess to drip down sides. KEEP REFRIGERATED. Serve withing 3 or 4 days. Serves 8-10.

BUTTERMILK FUDGE CAKE

- ¼-cup ho black coffee
- ½-cup unsweetened dry cocoa
- ½-cup oil
- 1 cup real buttermilk
- 1½-tsp baking soda

BAKE-SHOP SECRET
Inspired by Fred Sanders

- ½-tsp salt
- 1 TB vanilla extract
- 2 eggs
- 2 cups sugar
- 2 cups all-purpose flour

As given beat 1st 2 ingredients & then each remaining ingredient as listed, beating well with each addition. Pour batter into greased 9x13x2" pan. Bake 375F- 40 mins or till tester inserted into center comes out clean. Cool & frost. FUDGE CAKE FROSTING - Heat together 1-lb container ready-to-spread chocolate frosting & 1 cup semi-sweet morsels - stirring constantly, med-heat, till smooth. Spread over the cooled cake. Sprinkle with chopped walnuts. Serves 8 to 10

Gloria Pitzer's MAKE ALIKE RECIPES

SUGAR-FREE RASPBERRY Or Strawberry Pie

- 1 qt water
- 5 TB cornstarch
- 2 TB sugar-free lemonade powder
- Large box (8-serving size) Raspberry OR Strawberry sugar-free Jell-O powder
- 12-oz bag frozen (unthawed) raspberries or strawberries without any sugar added clearly on the label
- 9" or 10" baked pie shell - warm or cooled
- 2 envelopes Sweet Pretenders sugar-free whipped topping mix
- HALF of small box raspberry or strawberry sugar-free Jell-O powder to use as dusting garnish over top

In blendcer, high speed, combine 1st 4 ingredients, till it is smooth. Pour into medium saucepan. With wire whisk stir constantly on high till comes to boil (3 to 4 mins). Let boil ½-min still stirring. Remove at once from heat before it can scorch. Stir in frozen berries. Allow to cool in pan 30 mins. It will be soupy at first. Don't dispair! It should thicken a bit as it cools. Pour then carefully into pie shell. Let stand about an hour longer to thicken even more so that you can then transfer it carefully to refrigerator. In 3 or 4 hours when filling firms up a bit, apply prepared whipped topping & dust in additional Jell-O powder. Tape up the pkg of remaining Jell-O powder & put back into box & on the shelf to use when you make the pie again - And trust me, you will! Cut to serve 8 to 10.

SUGAR-FREE PINEAPPLE PIE

- 1 qt water
- 2 small boxes (4-serv size each) Hawaiian Pineapple Jell-O
- 5 TB cornstarch
- 1 TB sugar-free lemonade powder
- 15-oz can crushed pineapple - drained well
- 10" baked pei shell, warm or cooled
- 2 pkgs sguar-free whipped topping mix prepared per pkg.
- 8-oz (small can) pineapple rings, each cut in half, drained

In blender combine 1st 4 ingredients. Pour into saucepan & cook, stirring constantly with wire whisk till comes to boil & let boil ½-min, still stirring it. Remove from heat. Add crushed pineapple. Cool 1 hr. Pour into pie shell. Refrigerate 4 hrs. Apply prepared topping. Garnish around rim in the pineapple ring halves. Dust in a little more lemonade powder. Refrigerate at least 8 hrs before cutting to serve 8 to 10.

A Difference You Can Taste.

Gloria Pitzer's MAKE ALIKE RECIPES

Sugar-Free Lemon Pie WITH Jell-O

1-qt water
large box (8-serving size) sugar-free Lemon Jell-O
4 TB cornstarch
1 TB Sweet & Low sugar-free lemonade powder

Baked 10" pie shell (cooled or warm)
2 envelopes Sweet Pretenders sugar-free whipped topping mix
1 TB additional sugar-free lemonade powder

Into blender put 1st 4 ingredients. Blend high speed until smooth & pour at once into medium saucepan. Cook on high heat, stirring constantly with wire whisk, till comes to boil (4 to 5 mins). Continuing to stir constantly let boil ½-minute. Remove from heat. Let stand 20 mins in pan. (It will be soupy, but don't dispair!) Pour carefully into baked pie shell to the rim. Let stand another 30 mins or till begins to thicken enough that you can transfer it easily to refrigerator. Refrigerate 3 to 4 hrs or till filling is firm enough to hold topping, prepared per pkg directions and spread evenly over top. Dust in the additonal lemonade powder. Refrigerate to serve within 5 days. Serves 8 to 10 easily!

Sugar-Free Lemon Pie WITHOUT Jell-O

When you can't find Lemon flavored Jell-O powder do this:

1-qt water
3½-TB cornstarch
5½-TB lemonade sugar-free powder
2 envelopes Knox unflavored gelatine powder
2 tsp lemon extract
few drops yellow food coloring
10" baked pie shell warm or cooled

Put 1st 4 ingredients through blender high speed till well blended. Pour into med-saucepan, cooking on high, stirring with wire whisk constantly till comes to boil. Boil briskly, while still stirring, ½-min. Remove from heat. Stir in extract & food coloring. Pour into pie shell. Let stand 1 hour or till begins to thicken enough that you can transfer to refrigerator. Refrigerate 3 to 4 hrs or till filling is firm enough to be spread with 2 pkgs prepared sugar-free whipped topping mix & then dusted in 1 TB sugar-free lemonade powder. Keep refrigerated to cut & serve within 5 days. Serves 8 to 10 nicely.

NOTE: Either of these pies will cut nicely if refrigerated at least 8 to 10 hours. The 2nd version containing Knox unflavored gelatine, will cut best after 24 hours in refrig-

Gloria Pitzer's MAKE ALIKE RECIPES

THE PIE — perfection

KEY LIME PIE Inspired by Red Lobster's

Make a Graham cracker crust by combining 1½-c fine Graham cracker crumbs, ¼-c sugar, 6 TB soft butter or margarine. Press evenly over bottom & up sides of greased 9" pie pan. Bake 375F- 8 mins. Cool & prepare filling by beating together 14-oz can Eagle Brand Milk, 2 raw egg yolks, ½-cup lime juice, 3 mins high speed. Spread in cooled crust. Top with meringue made by beating together 2 egg whites till foamy, pinch salt & adding 7-oz marshmallow fluff till holds peaks. Bake 350F-15 mins or till meringue is golden brown. Chill before serving. Serves 8. (Do not freeze). Garnish with slice fresh lime.

ATTENTION PIE CRUST RECIPE in this book and in our other cookbooks. DO NOT use "light" margarine. Use only real butter or real margarine or crust will shrink during baking & come out tough as cardboard!

SIMPLE!

FAT-FREE (and/or Sugar-Free) Pie ——————— no-fat

Omit any butter or margarine called for in sugar-free pie filling recipes. Soon as you remove filling from heat, per recipes in this issue, wipe inside surface of 9" pie pan in a bit of hot prepared filling, smearing it evenly with rubber bowl scraper or your fingers. Then dust evenly in ½-cup very fine cornflakes crumbs, shaking out excess. Refrigerate coated pie pan while you allow filling to cool 10 mins before adding that lemonade powder. Fill crumb coated pie pan, continuing as pie recipes otherwise direct. ———————

ZUCCHINI BREAD Inspired by Bill Knapp's 3 miniature loaves

Stir together in med-bowl: 9-oz box (1-layer size) yellow cake mix, small box (4-serving) instant vanilla pudding powder, 1 cup grated, unpeeled zucchini. Set aside. Into blender put ¼-cup oil, 2 eggs, 2/3 cup broken walnuts, ½-cup orange juice, ½-tsp cinnamon & dash nutmeg. Blend briefly just to combine & pour over dry mixture, beating med-speed of mixer till dry stuff is dissolved. Divide between 3 greased 1-lb foil loaf pans, placed on cookie sheet. Bake 350F- 40 mins or till tester inserted in centers comes out clean. Cool in pans on rack 1 hour.

The 1-lb loaf pans are miniature pans.

Gloria Pitzer's MAKE ALIKE RECIPES

CARAMEL DELITE COOKIES
(Inspired by The Girl Scout's version 1991)

This is a donut shaped rich cookie that is coated in a thin caramel topping, then coated lightly in finely chopped toasted coconut and coated on the backside with melted semi-sweet chocolate and streaked across the top with chocolate. In different areas this cookie is boxed under different names, I found. This is my version of "their" cookie!

1 cup butter
2/3 cup powdered sugar
1 whole egg
1 raw egg yolk
1 tsp coconut extract
½-cup finely chopped toasted coconut*
2½-cups all-purpose flour

In medium bowl cream butter on high speed of electric mixer, adding sugar gradually, till light & fluffy. Beat in egg & yolk & extract. Work in coconut & flour to smooth dough. Use a fourth of the dough at a time, forcing it through cookie press "donut-shape disc dispenser", placing 1" apart on ungreased baking sheets. Bake 400F-only 7 to 10 mins or until set but not browned. Remove from pan to cool on waxed paper. makes 5 dozen. When cookies are completely cool prepare caramel coating.

Caramel Coating:

In small saucepan bring 4 TB light corn syrup to boil & add 12-oz jar Smucker's caramel sundae topping (sometimes called "hot caramel topping"). Lower heat to medium and stir mixture constantly till comes back to a boil. Boil 1 minute. Remove at once from heat. Using tip of sharp knife, lift cookies, one at a time, from the hole in center of each, into caramel mixture, coating each cookie lightly but evenly. Prop cookies upright between the wires of a pie rack, placed over cookie sheet to catch excess caramel dripping off. Quickly, before caramel sets dust cookies in toasted coconut. When air-dried arrange on jelly roll pan in single layer, in which you have spread 12-oz pkg semi-sweet morsels, melted over hot water till smooth. Removed coated cookies to greased waxed paper to set & cool.

(*) Oven Toast Coconut - for this cookie finely mince 7-oz flaked coconut in blender first. Spread it evenly over ungreased jelly roll pan & broiler toast, 6" from broiler heat, few minutes, **watching it closely so it won't burn!** Stir often till lightly browned. Quickly dump toasted coconut into cold bowl so it won't continue to brown in its own heat.

STREUSSEL CRUST
Is made by crushing fully baked crust into crumbs & evenly sprinkle it on top of filled pie.

DOUBLE CRUST
Is made by patting out dough per recipe below on greased wax paper lined 9" plate & inverting it over filled pie, peeling off paper, crimping rim & baking fully.

NO ROLLING PIN BUTTER CRUST

In 1½-qt mixing bowl using mixer on high speed, beat together ¼-lb butter, melted & still warm, 1 cup all-purpose flour, 1 TB sugar, 1 tsp salt & ¼-tsp cinnamon, beating 30-seconds just till combined. Work quickly while it's warm or crust may become crumbly. Pat it out quickly over bottom & up sides of a 9" Pam-sprayed pie pan. Do not prick the crust, tho. Bake 375F 18 mins or 'till well-browned. Cool & fill. FOR BAKED FILLING always partially bake crust at 375F- 6 min before adding filling & then bake per filling recipe.

Gloria Pitzer's MAKE ALIKE RECIPES

APPLE COBBLER Inspired by Keystone Kelly's-Ft. Erie, Ontario
Line 4 greased oven-proof soup bowls in our "No Rolling Pin Pie Crust" & bake 375F- 15 min or till browned. Fill with canned apple pie filling. Sprinkle top of each with Streussel Crust mixture (see Index). Keep warm in 275F- oven up to 30 mins before serving. ─────────────

FRENCH SILK PIES - Prepare any flavor Cook & Serve pudding as box directs. Soften 1 envelope unflavored gelatine in ¼ cup cold water till mushy. Stir at once into hot pudding as you remove it from heat. Also stir in 1 cup chocolate chips into chocolate pudding, butterscotch morsels into butterscotch pudding & 4-oz Alpine White Chocolate into vanilla.

OATMEAL RAISIN NUT COOKIES Inspired by Elias Big Boy

4 TB sour cream	1 tsp vanilla
1 egg	½-cup quick-cooking rolled oats
½-cup granulated sugar	1-2/3 cups Bisquick
3 TB Crisco	1½-cups raisins
1 tsp pumpkin pie spice	2/3 cup chopped walnuts
1 TB instant coffee powder	

As listed beat 1st 7 ingredients together well. Put rolled oats through blender till quite fine. Add with Bisquick to 1st mixture. Batter will be rich, smooth & thick. Work in raisins & walnuts. Use rounded TB dough 2" apart on Pam-sprayed cookie sheets. Grease bottom of glass once & dip into sugar, pressing down each spoonful of dough slightly. Bake at 400F- exactly 6 minutes. Cookies will not brown but should be set. Cool on baking sheets 2 mins. Remove gently to paper towels. Makes 2½-dozen cookies.

CASHEW NOUGAT COOKIES Inspired by Archway's

½-lb butter	1 TB vanilla
½-lb margarine	4 cups all-purpose flour
6 TB powdered sugar	3 cups chopped cashews
6 TB granulated sugar	2 more cups powdered sugar for later

Cream butter & margarine in lg mixing bowl, electric mixer high speed, 5 mins or till light & fluffy. Beat in sugars, vanilla 2 mins. Little at time beat in flour till smooth. Remove beaters. Work in cashews. Refrigerate dough 1 hour covered. Shape dough into 1" balls. Place 2" apart on ungreased cookie sheets. Bake 325F- 22 mins or till set but NOT browned. Cool on baking sheets 2 mins. Then roll each in the last 2 cups of powdered sugar, coating lightly but evenly. Cool on paper towels. Makes 6 dozen.

Gloria Pitzer's MAKE ALIKE RECIPES
ORANGE NUT BREAD Inspired by Bill Knapp's

9-oz box yellow cake mix (1-layer size)
small box (4-serving size) instant vanilla pudding
2 eggs
4 TB liquid margarine
1 tsp orange extract
½-cup orange juice
½-cup broken walnuts

Smells wonderful while it's in the oven!

Family Secret

Dump dry cake mix & dry pudding powder into medium mixing bowl. Set aside. Into blender put all remaining ingredients -even the walnuts). Blend a few seconds, just to combine thoroughly. Pour into dry cake mix mixture & beat with electric mixer just till dry ingredients are completely moistened & batter is smooth. Spread batter evenly in Pam-sprayed Pyrex bread loaf dish (22x11x6cm). Bake at 325F- 55 min to an hour or till tester inserted into center comes out clean. Cool in baking dish on rack 1 hr before removing to slice. Makes 1 loaf. Slice before freezing.

CHOCOLATE CAKE (Sour Milk Fudge Cake)
Inspired by Bill Knapp's

Into small skillet using wire whisk, combine over medium heat: 1 egg, ½-cup whole milk, 2/3 cup sugar, 4-squares (1-oz each) unsweetened baking chocolate. When smooth & it just comes to boil, remove from heat. Let cool. Meanwhile in medium bowl, using electric mixer, beat together ¼-lb butter or margarine, 1 cup sugar, 2 tsp vanilla, 2 eggs, 1 tsp baking soda, ½-tsp salt, 1 cup sour milk*, the cooled chocolate mixture, 2 cups flour. Beat 5 minutes. Scrape down sides & bottom of bowl often. Batter will be smooth & thick & rippled. Spread batter evenly in greased 9x13x2" pan & bake 350F- 35 to 40 mins or till tests done. OR divide equally between 2 greased & floured 8" or 9" layer pans. Bake 350F- ALSO 35 to 40 mins or till tester inserted into center comes out clean. Cool in pan on rack 30 mins & apply SPECIAL FROSTING (follows).

*SOUR MILK: Place 2 TB vinegar in 8-oz cup & add just enough milk to make 1-cup. (8-oz)

SPECIAL FROSTING For Chocolate Cake - In medium saucepan on medium heat stir together a 1-lb container of ready-to-spread chocolate frosting & 1 cup semi-sweet chocolate morsels. When melted & smooth, spread over cooled cake. Sprinkle top with chopped walnuts. Serves 8 to 10 beautifully. Freezes well to serve within 6 months.

Gloria Pitzer's MAKE ALIKE RECIPES

SUGAR-FREE FEATHERY FUDGE CAKE

This cake has the texture of "real" cake! Light & feathery!

I felt that recipe was okay but not as good as it could be. So after working, and re-working it, I found a way to increase the moistness and make the frosting easier to prepare...

The Cake:

1/2-tsp baking soda	2 raw egg whites
1 cup milk	beaten till foamy
1/3-cup mayonnaise	1/2-cup Nestles sugar-free
1/4-cup applesauce	chocolate QUIK powder
2 TB sour cream	2 1/4-cups self-rising flour

In mixing bowl using electric mixer to combine on medium speed, beat all but last 2 ingredients well —adding 1 item at a time, beating well after each addition. Beat in QUIK till dissolves and then flour till it is smooth. Spread batter evenly into Pam-sprayed Pyrex 8 1/2"x12x2" baking dish & bake at 350F- 25-30 mins or till tester inserted into center comes out clean. Cake will crack around edges during baking. Soon as out of the oven, let it cool on wire rack & spray top of cake evenly but lightly in Pam. Prepare topping.

SUGAR-FREE CAKE TOPPING

As box directs prepare <u>2 pkgs Cook & Serve</u> chocolate pudding. Upon removing from heat beat in <u>1 tsp liquid artificial sweetener with wire whisk (or use 4 packets dry Equal.) Spread warm pudding over warm cake.</u> Let it cool about 10 mins before cutting into 12 pieces. Refrigerate leftovers to use in a few days. Yes, it freezes well, too.

SUGAR FREE RECIPE

PUMPKIN SEEDS - Salty

One of the simple autumn snacks that never come out just like those you can buy in the boxes at the candy counters is a matter of technique rather than recipe. Dissolve 1 cup table salt in 4 cups water over medium heat in a 2-qt saucepan. Bring it to a boil to be sure the salt is completely dissolved. Pour it then into a larger kettle that will accomodate it nicely plus 4 cups tap water. Add the cleaned seeds of your pumpkins to measure about 2 cups. Let these stand overnight or at least 12 to 15 hours. Then beat 2 egg whites till foamy, but not stiff. Coat the seeds in the egg whites and arrange on a brown paper lined cookie sheet in single layer and dust liberally in salt. Bake at 275F—for about 45 minutes to an hour, or till the surface of the seeds appears dry. For a heavier coating, you can dip the seeds back into more beaten egg white and dust again in salt, returning to the oven till dry enough to please you.

Gloria Pitzer's MAKE ALIKE RECIPES

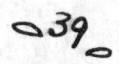

MILKY WAY CAKE OR SNICKERS BAR CAKE

It's not a cakelike-cake, but more like a crust with bits of candy bars melted in it. A delightful departure from the usual!

18-oz box yellow cake mix
2 boxes (4-serving size each) instant vanilla pudding
2 cups Quick Cooking Quaker Oats (used dry)
1½-cups real mayonnaise
4 Milky Way or Snickers candy bars (2.15-oz each)
½-cup powdered sugar

Into large mixing bowl, dump dry cake mix, dry pudding powder & oats. Stir to combine & work in mayonnaise with electric mixer on high speed till you have a firm but moist dough. Pat dough out lightly but evenly over bottom of greased 9x13 or 10x13 or two 9-inch square pans. With scissors, snip candy bars into bits & press gently into dough evenly over top. Bake 300F- about 35 mins or till "set" & dry & puffy looking. Cool on rack & while still warm dust top in the powdered sugar. Let cool 30 mins before cutting into squares to serve several safely.───────────

CRUMB CAKE Inspired by Sara Lee's (1970's)

2 cups sifted flour
2 cups packed light brown sugar
½-cup margarine

1 egg well beaten
½-cup additional flour
2 tsp baking powder
1 tsp cinnamon
3/4-cup milk

Mix 1st 3 ingredients till crumbly. Set aside ½-cupful & to the remaining crumb mixture add remaining ingredients as given above. Beat well, mixer on low speed. Spread evenly in a greased 8" square pan. Sprinkle reserved crumbs over top and bake 350F- for 35 to 40 mins or till toothpick inserted into center comes out clean. Dust warm cake in powdered sugar before cutting to serve 9 nicely.───────────

BUNDT CAKE FROM SCRATCH

In lg mixing bowl combine: 2¼-c flour, 2-c sugar, ½-tsp salt, ½-tsp baking soda, 1 tsp vanilla, 1 c butter or margarine, at room temp, 1 c sour cream, 3 eggs. Beat 3 mins med-speed and spread batter in greased 12-cup Bundt pan. Bake 325F-1 hour- or till tester inserted through cake comes out clean. Cool in pan upright 45 mins. Invert onto plate & drizzle with icing.

THE "ULTRA"

Unlike other alternatives

NEW

Gloria Pitzer's MAKE ALIKE RECIPES

NEST-LEASED CRUNCH BARS

Inspired by the candy bar of a similar name...
In top of double boiler over gently simmering water, melt 6 bars (1¼-oz ea) NESTLES milk chocolate & 1 cup miniature marshmallows, stirring till perfectly smooth. Gradually stir in 4 cups slightly crushed RICE KRISPIES to coat evenly. Quickly spread mixture evenly in greased jelly roll pan. Let stand at room temperature till firm. Cut with pizza wheel into bars 1½"x4" each. Do not refrigerate. Store in covered container at room temperature. Makes 9 bars.

STRAWBERRY CANDIES

Inspired by the popular marzipan candies of the holidays.

It's a 'secret'!

14-oz can Eagle Brand Milk
14-oz flaked moist coconut
large box strawberry Jell-O powder
1 cup ground blanched almonds
1 tsp almond extract
Few drops red food coloring
1 tube ready-to-use green tinted frosting with tip

Combine Eagle Brand Milk & coconut with only 1/3 cup of Jell-O powder. Work in almonds, extract & enough red food coloring to give color of strawberries to mixture. Refrigerate till firm enough to shape into strawberry-looking pieces. Allow 1 TB mixture for each. Roll to coat each piece in remaining Jell-O powder in shallow dish. Coat each one lightly but evenly. Arrange on waxed paper lined cookie sheet. Refrigerate several hours or till firm. Create hulls for berries by applying a bit of green frosting with rosette tip to top of each candy. Refrigerate in covered container to use in a week. Do NOT freeze, please. Makes about 40 pieces

MAMIE EISENHOWER'S FUDGE

Here's the recipe for Mrs. Eisenhower's million dollar fudge that lured the 2nd Lieutenant who later became The President of the U.S. Bring to a boil 4½-cups sugar, dash salt, 2 TB butter, 12-oz can Pet milk. Boil 6 mins. Place 12-oz semi-sweet morsels in bowl with 12-oz German Sweet Chocolate in bits, 16-oz marshmallow cream & 2 cups chopped walnuts. Pour boiling mixture over chocolate mixture, beating well till blended. Spread evenly in greased 9 in. square pan. Refrigerate 24 hr before cutting into pieces.

Gloria Pitzer's MAKE ALIKE RECIPES

YUMMY BARS Chocolate Coated Wafer Cookies

This recipe originally came from Betty Thomas's "Cracker Barrel" a recipe newsletter, in which Betty published recipes taken from her show with Radio Station KDTH in Dubuque, Iowa 52001. To subscribe to the newsletter, send Betty $4 for a year of monthly issues.

14 Club Crackers
¼-lb (1 stick) butter or margarine
1 cup fine Graham Cracker crumbs
   (16 square crackers put through blender till powdered)

¾-cup packed brown sugar
½-cup granulated sugar
1/3 cup milk

6-oz pkg chocolate chips
2/3 cup peanut butter

keep her's

Arrange 7 of the Club Crackers to fit into bottom of greased 9x12 inch pan, breaking up the crackers to make them fit into a single layer. In 1½-qt saucepan on medium high, melt the butter or margarine and stir in the Graham Cracker crumbs, both sugars and milk. Cook, stirring this constantly till comes to a boil. Continue stirring constantly and let it boil very gently exactly 5 minutes. (Set your timer!) Remove then from heat at once and pour over crackers in that pan. At once arrange remaining Club Crackers in another layer over the caramel mixture. Melt chocolate chips with peanut butter in top of double boiler, over hot, not boiling water, till smooth and pour over cracker layer. Spread it around best you can before it has a chance to harden. Refrigerate about 10 minutes. Cut into bars. Keep these in the refrigerated, covered in plastic wrap, to use in a few days — although I doubt that they will last that long! Makes about 24 nice sized bars.

SNITCHER BARS CANDY BARS

If you like Snicker Bars — you'll love this understudy version.

LIKE NO OTHER

9¼-oz bag Brach's caramels
2 TB light Karo
2 TB water
2 bags (12-oz ea) semi-sweet chocolate chips
2 TB solid Crisco
1 TB peanut butter

1/3 cup light Karo syrup
3 TB margarine
3 TB peanut butter
1 tsp vanilla
Dash Salt
1-lb powdered sugar
2 cups shelled, skinless peanuts

In top double boiler over HOT (not boiling) water, melt till smooth the caramels, 2 TB Karo & water. In top of another double boiler over HOT —not boiling—water, melt chocolate chips, Crisco & 1 TB peanut butter. Stir till smooth. In medium mixing bowl using electric mixer, high speed, beat remaining Karo, margarine, remaining peanut butter, vanilla & salt till creamy. Dump in powdered sugar all at once. Beat till crumbly. Knead in bowl with hand sprayed in Pam or wiped with oil, kneading till smooth & firm. Place this mixture in plastic food bag & roll out in the bag to 10x15-inches. Set aside. Spray a 10x15x¾" jelly roll pan in Pam. Spread half of melted chocolate mixture evenly over bottom of pan. When firm, press rolled out & kneaded candy mixture into place over the chocolate layer. Spread warm melted caramel over that. Sprinkle peanuts evenly over that. Using rubber bowl scraper, spread rest of melted chocolate over top. Refrigerate an hour or till firm enough to cut into 20 bars, 1"wide. Use pizza wheel or sharp knife to cut bars.

Gloria Pitzer's MAKE ALIKE RECIPES

Eureka! NEW

PEPPER ITCH ARMS MINT MALANO COOKIES
1 cup butter
½-cup sugar
1 egg
1 tsp almond extract
2 cups + 2 TB sifted flour (sift before measuring)
1/8 tsp salt

Cream butter till fluffy using electric mixer (3 mins) high-speed. Gradually beat in sugar & then the egg & almond. Beat med-speed to blend well & then add flour on low & salt till incorporated. Put through cookie press, using oval or round plain-unscalloped disc. Drop cookies 2" apart on ungreased cookie sheets. Bake 375 oven 10 mins (Do not brown these). NOTE: If you do not have a cookie press drop dough with measuring teaspoon onto baking sheets as directed for using the cookie press & then flatten each slightly into a circle or oval with spatula. Wipe cookie sheets of all traces of butter between bakings. Dough will not stick to sheets if pans are too warm or too greasy. Makes 4 dozen.
MALANO FILLING:
12-oz pkg semi-sweet chips
1-oz solid bitter chocolate
2 TB melted paraffin
2 tsp peppermint extract
dash of salt
Combine in top of double boiler over boiling water & stir till melted & smooth. Spread a tspful of this over flat side of one baked cookie at a time quickly covering it with plain flat side of another cookie. Makes 2 dozen.

DE-CLASSIFIED

FIG NEW FUN BARS

The dough is prepared first and while it is being chilled for an hour, you prepare the filling

Cream together till light and fluffy
½-cup butter
½-cup margarine
½-cup sugar a spoonful at a time
Then beat in:
½-cup honey
2 large eggs
Then a little at a time mix in:
4½-cups self rising flour

Blend thoroughly and refrigerate 1 hr.

Prepare the filling:
1-lb can drained figs cut small
½-cup sugar
½-cup black cold tea
Place in top of double boiler over simmering water, cooking and stirring often till sugar dissolves.

Add:
½-cup finely ground pecans
¼-tsp cinnamon
1/16 tsp powdered ginger
Blend well and allow to cool 15 minutes

Roll dough on floured surface ¼" thick. Shape the piece of dough so that it is about 5" wide and as long as necessary to achieve that thickness & width.

Spread filling down center of the strip of dough. Fold it in half & pinch seam to seal in filling. Slice into 3" long bars. Arrange 1" apart on foil covered cookie sheets, greasing foil lightly and use shiny side up. Bake at 400 degrees about 8 to 10 minutes or till delicately browned. Do not overbake these. Then let them cool and store them in airtight container along with one fresh apple to keep them softened and fresh. They freeze indefinitely. Makes 6 doz.

Gloria Pitzer's MAKE ALIKE RECIPES

43

Soft Serve FROZEN DESSERT SNOWSTORM

THE FAMOUS BLIZZARD INSPIRED THIS!

iF YOU HAVE NEVER HAD a Blizzard at your favorite Dairy Queen, you don't know what you've been missing! Just because there are only a few simple ingredients involved, though, don't underestimate the care you must take in recreating this marvelous dessert in your own kitchen, using our recipe!

IT WAS WARREN PIERCE of WJR Radio in Detroit who first sparked my interest in trying to imitate this yummy concoction at home. And this is the recipe that I shared with Warren and his listeners.

1 quart vanilla ice cream
¼-cup Hershey's Syrup
2 TB non-dairy creamer powder (like Creamora)
2 pkgs (1.6-oz each) M&M candies
 or any of the suggested candies given below - chopped fine

Have the ice cream slightly softened at room temperature, so that you can spoon it easily into pieces each about the size of an egg. Place these in a 1½-quart mixing bowl, adding syrup & creamer powder & beat with electric mixer on lowest speed till completely combined and smooth. Remove beaters. Stir in chopped candies. Divide mixture at once between 3 cups (10-oz each). If mixture begins to melt too quickly, depending on humidity and temperature of the room, place mixture in freezer about 15 minutes or till you can serve it with a spoon easily. Serves 3 adequately, 2 foolishly!

NOTE ON CHOPPING CANDIES:
 The easiest way to chop the candies is to lightly tap each candy bar or package of candies with a hammer, b-e-f-o-r-e you unwrap them!
 OR you can remove 1/3 cup of the finished ice cream mixture from the mixing bowl and place in your blender with the unwrapped candies. Blend only a few seconds on "grind" or high speed till well chopped. Then stir into finished ice cream, per directions above.

SUGGESTED CANDIES TO ADD:

Butterfinger Candy Bar
Heath Candy Bar
M&M Candies
M&M Peanut Candies
Reese's Pieces
Nestles Crunch Bar
6-oz (1 cup) chocolate chips
1 cup slightly crushed
 vanilla wafer cookies
1 cup slightly crushed
 Hydrox chocolate cookies
1 cup chopped
 chocolate covered cherries
½-cup diced, drained,
 red Maraschino cherries

Gloria Pitzer's MAKE ALIKE RECIPES

CHOCOLATE CHIP COOKIES
Inspired by Elias Bros Big Boy

Prepare cookie recipe below, but use only 3½-cups flour instead of 4 cups & omit coconut flavoring and butter flavoring entirely. Use chopped walnuts instead of the pecans and continue as recipe otherwise directs for preparation, baking at 375F– 12 mins without OVERbaking, please. Cool few mins on baking sheets before removing to paper towels.

right on target

CHOCOLATE CHIP COOKIES
(Sanders' Style of the early 1950's)

1/3 cup Crisco Oil
½-lb butter (2 sticks) or margarine
1 cup firmly packed light brown sugar
1 cup granulated sugar
2 large eggs
1 tsp baking soda
½-tsp baking powder
¼-tsp salt
½-tsp vanilla extract
½-tsp coconut extract
1 tsp butter flavoring (optional)
4 cups all-purpose flour
1 cup finely chopped pecans
12-oz pkg semi-sweet chocolate morsels

TEMPTATION

As listed combine ingredients in large mixing bowl, beating well with each addition, using electric mixer, medium speed, switching to mixing spoon to add morsels. Prepare cookie sheet (*) & drop dough 2" apart on prepared sheet, using level measuring TB for each cookie. Then flatten each mound of dough slightly with 2 fingers, shaping into rounds about 3/8" thick. Bake at 400F—exactly 10 minutes or at 375F—exactly 12 mins—or just till delicately, light golden in color. Do NOT overbake. Cool on baking sheet 2 mins. Transfer to paper towels till cookies are completely cooled. Makes 6 dozen.

(*)Spray cookie sheet in Pam. Place in 400F—oven 3 to 4 mins or till Pam turns brown. Wipe browned Pam off with paper towel, leaving light but even film. Apply dough to prepared warm cookie sheet per recipe. Do NOT reapply Pam to cookie sheet. This process is good for all 6 dozen cookies without regreasing cookie sheets.

ITALIAN SHORTBREAD COOKIE BARS
Like The Fernhill Country Club

SHORTBREAD COOKIE BARS are a favorite Italian pastry that I find at almost every event catered by fine Italian chefs. Recently at my husband's school reunion, I discovered the absolute-best Italian Shortbread Cookie Bars, and even a many-year friendship with the owner of the country club, could not get me the original recipe! So I tried several things I suspected might work—and one of them did!

2 eggs
1 cup granulated sugar
1 tsp almond extract
1 tsp vanilla extract
3 TB solid Crisco
3 TB real butter
(or butter flavored Crisco)
3 cups Bisquick

6-oz pkg (1 cupful) semi-sweet morsels

Preheat oven to 300F—. Spray a jelly roll pan in Pam. In 1½-qt mixing bowl with electric mixer on medium, beat eggs & sugar till light & fluffy, adding each additional ingredient, beating well after each. Clean the dough from the beaters & use wet hands to pat the dough lightly but evenly over bottom of prepared pan. Bake at 300F—(very low) for 25 mins. (Delicately light golden—not browned). At once put the morsels into blender, grinding till in crumbs & sprinkle immediately over surface of hot cookie dough soon as you remove from oven. Cool 20 mins. Score ¼" from edge of pan, on all 4 sides & discard this much before cutting remaining portion into 1"x2" bars. Refrigerate in covered containers to use in a week or so or freeze to thaw & serve within 3 months. (3 dozen).

SNOW CONES

Place 2 trays of ice cubes in center of smooth towel, covering with half of towel & hammer into crushed bits that you pack into small Dixie paper cups. Keep in the freezer, each one covered with plastic wrap, secured with rubber bands. Just before serving, drizzle each cupful of crushed ice with about 2 TB fruit-flavored pancake syrup (Smucker's suggested).

THE HEALTH BUZZWORD THESE DAYS ISN'T "LOW-CAL," IT'S "LOW-FAT."

FAT-FREE STRAWBERRY ICE CREAM
Inspired by 31 Flavors

2 pints (4 cupsful) fresh strawberries in halves lengthwise
10-oz pkg miniature marshmallows
1 TB milk
1 TB lemon juice
½-tsp strawberry extract or flavoring

Blend strawberries in blender, high speed, till smooth. Set aside. Melt marshmallows & milk in small pan over med-heat till smooth, or Micro melt. Gradually beat berries into marshmallow mixture, then lemon juice & extract, beating just to combine. Pour into 9" square baking pan or freezer container & freeze about 2 hrs or till almost solid. Break it up & beat with electric mixer in chilled bowl till smooth. Freeze again till firm enough to scoop. Makes about 1 quart.

SUGAR-FREE FROZEN CUSTARD (Soft Serve)

Into blender put 2 cups milk, 2 TB cornstarch, 3 raw egg yolks, 2 TB butter or margarine. Blend till smooth high speed. Pour into medium saucepan & cook, stirring constantly on medium heat till smooth & thickened like a pudding. Remove from heat. Cool & refrigerate till icey cold. Beat in 2 packets Sweet & Low or more to taste, plus ½-pint heavy cream whipped with pinch salt & 2 packets Sweet & Low till it holds its shape when beaters are removed. Fold whipped cream in carefully with rubber bowl scraper so you don't reduce volume too much. Set aside. Beat 3 egg whites till stiff with 2 packets Sweet & Low. Fold into cream mixture with lowest speed of mixer. Freeze till firm enough to scoop. Break up & beat again with electric mixer till smooth & creamy. Then freeze for last time till firm enough to scoop. Keep tightly covered. Makes 3 pints.

Gloria Pitzer's MAKE ALIKE RECIPES

YOGURT HOMEMADE — YOGURT
Inspired by Dannon's

Bring 1-qt milk to boil, stirring frequently on med-heat. Allow to cool to 100F- using candy thermometer. Skim off any skin forming on top. Add 3 TB plain commercial yogurt & place in plastic container with tight-fitting lid, wrapping in several thick bath towels or an electric blanket - low temp for 5 hours. Don't let it overstablize. When has become smooth & custardlike, refrigerate. Makes 1-quart.—

FROZEN YOGURT Inspired by TCBY

In small saucepan bring 2¼-cups skim milk to boil. Remove from heat. Let stand till lukewarm. Sprinkle 1 envelope dry unflavored gelatine over milk. Stir in vigorously with wire whisk till dissolved. Then stir in 1 TB vanilla, ½-cup sugar, dash salt. Return to heat. Cook on low heat, stirring constantly 5 minutes or till gelatine & sugar is dissolved. Remove from heat. Cool completely. Stir in 1½-cups plain yogurt & ¼-cup light corn syrup. Refrigerate mixture covered 8 hours. Pour into ice cream maker & prepare per manufacturer's directions as for vanilla ice cream. When completed, remove from machine to freezer container & freeze 1 hour to let flavors blend. Makes 1 quart.

SUGAR-FREE PEACH ICE CREAM
Inspired by 31 Flavors (Basket & Ribbons)

1-lb can sliced cling peaches undrained (no sugar added)
6-oz orange juice
1 cup whipped, heavy cream
1 TB liquid sweetener (Sweet 10 preferred)

Into blender put undrained peaches & orange juice. Blend 1 minute to break up but not puree. Pour into mixing bowl & add whipped cream, extract & sweetener. Combine well. Cover tightly. Place in freezer 30 mins. POUR INTO ICE CREAM MAKER & CONTINUE PER MANUFACTURER'S DIRECTIONS OR freeze it till firm enough to scoop. Break up & beat with electric - mixer till fluffy & light. Return to freezer till firm enough to scoop. Makes about a pint. (Recipe can be doubled) (Almond extract can be added to taste as 5th ingredient.)

Gloria Pitzer's MAKE ALIKE RECIPES

ICE CREAM CONES HOMEMADE

2 egg whites
3/4-cup powdered sugar
dash salt
1/4-tsp vanilla extract
1/2-cup all-purpose flour
1/4-cup butter, melted & cooled

Beat egg whites till quite stiff. Gradually fold in sugar & salt & vanilla. Use low speed of mixer to combine thoroughly & then work in flour litle at a time to smooth batter. Fold in cooled, melted butter. Preheat a "Krumkake" iron or other similar stovetop iron over moderate surface burner. Put only 1½-TB batter into preheated iron. Close carefully. Don't squeeze lid too tightly. Heat 2 mins & turn iron to bake on other side 2 mins longer or till you can check the inside & see that it is light beige in color. Remove from iron. Place around a cone form till it cools. Fill delicately with ice cream. Makes 6 small cones.

LEMON SORBET (Sherbet)
Inspired by 31 Flavors

CLASSY

Mix together well 1 cup sugar, 3 TB lemon juice, 2 tsp grated lemon rind. Slowly add 1 pint light cream & 2 dropps yellow food coloring to tint it lightly. Pour into freezer container. Freeze till firm enough to scoop. Makes 1½-pints.

HOT BUTTERSCOTCH SUNDAE Topping

If you love Sanders' Hot Butterscotch Sundae Topping that was a weekly "must" for fans 30 years ago at their downtown Detroit Woodward Avenue store, you will adore this recipe!

12-oz pkg Butterscotch Morsels
6-oz box Nestle's Bar White Chocolate
14-oz can Eagle Brand Milk
14-oz light corn syrup (Karo)
½-lb butter or margarine (2 sticks)

Combine all ingredients exactly as listed, in top of double boiler, over very h-o-t but NOT boiling water. Stir frequently until melted and smooth, and then allow mixture to cook stirring only occasionally for 30 minutes. Use portable electric mixer to beat mixture before removing from over hot water, just till smooth—OR better yet, put mixture through blender, high speed—turning off motor to clean away mixture from blades—till smooth. Refrigerate to rewarm over hot water—or on low temp in Microwave, to spoon over ice cream. Makes about a quart. Freeze in small portions to thaw and rewarm within a year.

DELICIOUS

Gloria Pitzer's MAKE ALIKE RECIPES

COFFEECAN ICE CREAM Inspired by 31 Flavors

Totally Unique Ice Cream

1 cup heavy whipping cream
1 cup milk
1 egg, well beaten
½-cup granulated sugar
1 TB vanilla extract

20 cups crushed ice
1½-cups Kosher Salt or Ice Cream Freezing Salt

Put 1st 5 ingredients into blender, high speed, 30 seconds or till combined well. Pour into ungreased 1-lb coffeecan with tight fitting lid. Secure lid tightly in place. Into a larger - 3-lb coffeecan arrange about 2 cups crushed ice over bottom of can & set the smaller can containing cream mixture into it, centering it. Pack space between small can & the outer larger can with crushed ice, always sprinkling each cupful of the ice with ¼-cup of the salt, then another cup of ice & another ¼-cup salt till space is well packed with it. Secure lid tightly in place on larger outer can & roll the can back & forth on flat surface for 10 mins. (Set timer!) You may wish to have an assisting pair of hands ready to relieve you during this rolling time - or give to the kids to do while they're watching TV. After the 10 min rolling time is up, remove lid from large can. Hold small can in place as you tip both cans to drain off any melted ice into sink. Repack it with the cupful ice/¼-cup salt as directed above & secure lid again. Roll back & forth 10 mins longer. Remove lid of both cans, checking texture of ice cream. If thick enough for your liking, serve at once. Makes about 2½-cups ice cream.

CHOCOLATE ICE CREAM - when you combine cream in blender with other ingredients, substitute chocolate milk for reg'l milk & add ¼-cup Hershey's chocolate syrup. Continue as otherwise directed above.

STRAWBERRY ICE CREAM - when you remove lid of large can to drain off any melted ice at end of 1st 10 mins as directed above, stir in 8 to 10 frozen, whole strawberries, each sliced in half & unthawed. Continue as otherwise directed in recipe above.

(For more intense strawberry flavor, add 2 TB Nestles Quik strawberry drink powder to other ingredients in blender in 1st step of recipe given above.)

Gloria Pitzer's MAKE ALIKE RECIPES

CUSTARD — Cooked GENTLE CUSTARD

3 eggs
2 cups milk
½-cup sugar
3 TB cornstarch
¼-tsp salt
1 tsp vanilla
2 TB margarine or butter
¼-tsp nutmeg
½-cup (two boxes -1-oz each) golden raisins

Put all but raisins into blender & blend high speed half a minute or till smooth. Pour mixture into 2-qt Teflon lined saucepan. On med-high heat, stir constantly for about 5 minutes or till mixture begins to thicken and become smooth. Remove from heat. Let stand a few minutes. Divide equally between 5 or 6 small dessert dishes. Chill or serve warm right away

POTATO CHIP COOKIES

Cream together till fluffy: 1 cup of butter, 1/2 cup sugar, 1 tsp vanilla. Work in 2 cups flour, 1/2 cup crushed potato chips, 1/2 cup chopped pecans. Drop by tspful onto ungreased baking sheet 2" apart. Flatten with greased & sugar-coated glass bottom. Bake at 350F—about 10 to 12 minutes or till delicately browned. Makes 5 dozen.

LEMONADE HOMEMADE

1 cup lemon juice (about 6 lemons)
1 cup sugar (or 20 packets Nutra Sweet)
1 quart cold water
1 fresh lemon sliced paper thin
2 trays of ice cubes

Put it all together in a 2-qt beverage container or pitcher. Serves 6 nicely.

(NOTE: 1 packet of Equal -Nutra-Sweet is equal to 2 tsp sugar.

SUGAR-FREE CHOCOLATE PECAN COOKIES

2 cups Bisquick
2/3 cup Brown Sugar Twin
1 box (4-serving size) sugar-free instant butterscotch pudding
1 box (4-serving size) sugar-free instant chocolate pudding
4 TB butter or margarine melted & cooled
1 tsp vanilla
¼-cup mayonnaise
2½-oz chopped pecans

As listed mix all ingredients together, beating well after each addition. Drop dough by tspful onto ungreased baking sheets. Bake 350F—16 to 18 mins or till firm. Cool on pan 5 mins & then transfer to paper towels. Makes 4 dozen —at about 45 calories per cookie.

EGGNOG

Using the Gentle Custard as the basis of this Holiday Drink, I put 3 eggs into the blender with 2 cups milk, ½-cup sugar, 3 TB cornstarch and pinch of salt, blending about 10 seconds, till smooth. Then I poured it into a Teflon coated 2-qt saucepan and began stirring it over medium high till it thickened like a pudding. I took it off the heat at once and stirring in ½-tsp nutmeg, 3 TB butter (or margarine) and 1 tsp vanilla, using a wire whisk to blend it till smooth. I poured it into a refrigerator container. Covered it and chilled it about 2 hours. In the mean time I whipped 1 cup heavy whipping cream till it held its own shape in peaks when I lifted the beaters out. I then turned the beaters to low speed and beat in ½-cup powdered sugar. I folded this stiffly beaten sweetened cream into the chilled egg mixture till it was smooth. Turned it into a punch bowl and added 2-qts golden gingerale —preferably Vernor's if available. Then I served it in small cups to a dozen of our visiting neighbors and family one chilly Christmas Eve. If wish, you can add 1 cup light rum to the mixture in the punch bowl just before you serve it. Makes 12 to 15 lovely, warm servings.

Gloria Pitzer's MAKE ALIKE RECIPES

ITALIAN WEDDING CAKE
Inspired by Farmer Jack's

Prepare 1 recipe of our PERFECT LEMON LAYER CAKE but use 1 TB vanilla or almond extract instead of lemon extract, as given in that recipe. For a tier-cake, prepare the recipe twice, baking the 1st recipe in two 9" layer pans per recipe directions, but bake the 2nd recipe in FOUR 6" or 7" round layer pans. Assemble the layers applying frosting between the two 9" layers and then put THREE of the smaller layers together with frosting, cutting the 4th layer into a round that is 1" smaller in diameter than the other 3, using that as the top layer. Apply frosting to top and sides and decorate with ready to use tubes of vanilla icing with decorator's tubes or candy rosettes made by Betty Crocker, applied with dab of frosting to secure in place. This cake will serve 50

WEDDING CAKE FROSTING: Beat 8-oz very soft cream cheese till light & fluffy, using electric mixer medium speed. Beat in 4 TB butter or margarine till fluffy, then 1 tsp vanilla or almond extract & 1-lb powdered sugar, little at a time till creamy & smooth. Frosts a 3 layer 9" cake.

PERFECT POUNDCAKE Powdered Sugar
Inspired by Sara Lee's (1980)

Originally inspired by the "All-Butter Poundcake", which has been replaced now with a cholesterol-free version that is half as tasty, a far-cry from original goodness.

½-lb real butter or real margarine
2 cups powdered sugar
3 large eggs
1-2/3-cups flour
1 TB lemon extract or vanilla

Preheat oven to 325F-. Spray 8½" Pyrex loaf dish in Pam. Cream butter with powdered sugar, high speed of electric mixer, 5 mins. Add 1 egg & then a little flour, beating 2 mins. Add 2nd egg & half of remaining flour & beat 2 mins. Add 3rd egg & rest of flour & extract, beating 2 mins. Spread thick & creamy batter evenly in prepared loaf dish. Bake at 325F- for 65 mins or till tester inserted into center of loaf comes out clean of any wet batter. Cool in baking dish on wire rack 30 mins. Remove from dish. Slice ½" thick. makes 10 slices. Be sure to slice before freezing loaf.

Thaw to use within 6 months.

ELEGANT italian wedding cake

Gloria Pitzer's MAKE ALIKE RECIPES

Salads

— FAT-FREE DRESSING

HEALTHY IDEA

pasta that tastes as good as scratch

SPAGHETTI SALAD (Fat-Free Dressing)
Inspired by Ponderosa's Biggest Buffet

Break 8-oz pkg THIN spaghetti into 2" or 3" lengths as you drop them into rapidly boiling, slightly salted water in 2½-qt saucepan. Allow to simmer gently about 8-10 mins or till el dente (tender-to-the-bite). Drain & rinse in cold water, draining again. Combine pasta with a dressing made by combining: 1/3 cup vinegar, 1/3 cup water, 1/3 cup ketchup, 4 tsp sugar or 4 packets Sweet & Low or to taste. Add also 1 tsp dry minced onion, 1 rib celery minced fine, a few dill pickle chips minced fine, a dash of dry dill weed, 1 cup shredded Mozzarella, 1 ripe tomato, diced well, chopped green or black olives to taste if you wish. cover tightly & refrigerate several hours or overnight before serving. Serves 6 sensibly!

SEAFOOD PASTA SALAD

To the above recipe add 4 or 5 mock crab legs each cut into ½" pieces, 8-oz bag frozen, but thawed, cooked salad shrimp. Serves 6 to 8 adequately.

FRENCH DRESSING Inspired by Hedge's Wigwam

Remembering

Twenty years ago bottled salad dressings were basic-but wonderful! At Hedges' Wigwam, a unique cafeteria restaurant at what was then the corner of Woodward & 10 Mile in Royal Oak (Mich), there was served even before that, a sweet/tart orange colored dressing that I have never found anywhere since. The lifelike statues of Indians in front of Hedge'ws in warrior bonnets, pillared the entrance to one of the most outstanding eateries of the 1940's & 50's. From the slate water fall & gold fish pon at the end of the cafeteria line, to the heavy carved log tables & matching chairs, even the gift shop street-side with maple sugar delights for sale, it's never to be duplicated again.

10-oz can cream tomato soup	2 TB prepared mustard
8-oz malt vinegar	1 TB salt
8-oz corn oil	4 TB paprika
2/3 cup sugar	½-tsp black pepper

In blender combine high speed 1 min or till thoroughly & beautifully mixed. Refrigerate tightly covered to use in 90 days. Makes about 1 quart.

Gloria Pitzer's MAKE ALIKE RECIPES

HEALTHY FOOD The Chicken Salad of the '90s

CHICKEN SALAD WITH VINAIGRETTE DRESSING
Inspired by Little Teapot Restaurant - Pt. Huron, Mich)

Specialty Restaurant

A delightful whole meal salad, served with muffin or dinner roll, priced at $4.95 on the menu.

1/4th-of-a-head of lettuce in bite sized pieces
1 large ripe tomato, diced
1 cup finely cut fresh broccoli buds
1/4-cup grated carrot (on large whole of grater)
1 cup diced red cabbage
1/2-cup peeled finely diced cucumber
1/2-cup chopped pecans
1 boneless, skinless chicken breast cut into 1" wide strips & sauteed till tender in few tablespoons oil

THE VINAIGRETTE DRESSING:
2 TB red wine vinegar
2 TB oil
Salt & pepper to taste
4 TB water
3 TB sugar (or 6 packets of Sweet & Low)

Combine all ingredients as listed for the salad, arranging sauteed chicken strips over top. then saturate in combined dressing ingredients. Let salad stand 5 mins before serving to "wilt" the lettuce a bit. makes 1 generous meal-sized salad. (Does not keep well, so plan to serve it as-soon-as you prepare it. (Do not freeze, please!)

COLESLAW Inspired by Long John Silvers's
Combine 1 medium head cabbage in matchstick pieces & 1 cup milk with 2 carrots grated fine, 1 TB dry minced onion, 1 TB season salt, covered in refrigerator 1 hour. Drain well & add a dressing made by combining 2 c mayonnaise, 8-oz sour cream, 3 TB sugar, 1 tsp prepared mustard, 1 tsp celery seed. Cover & chill 24 hrs before serving. Serves 6 to 8 nicely.

CHI CHI INSPIRED HOUSE DRESSING
If you like the house dressing at Chi Chi's you'll love this make-alike. Into your blender, put equal parts Chi Chi's bottled Salsa & Catalina Dressing & blend high speed till smooth. (Our version of their salsa is on pg 106 of our FAMOUS FAVORITES book!) The other dressing on their salad bar can be made by blending 8-oz bottled Ranch with 1/4-cup bottled salsa smooth.

Gloria Pitzer's MAKE ALIKE RECIPES

Slaw Dressing
Cole Slaw

SALADS

SUZIE Q COLESLAW

Inspired by a 1950 restaurant at Woodward & 12 Mile in Royal Oak (Mich) where I grew up just a block away!

Combine 6 cups prepared cabbage, 1 cup finely shredded carrot, 3 TB dry minced onion with an 8-oz bottled Wishbone Italian Dressing, ½-cup corn oil, 3 TB lemon juice, 1 TB sugar plus dash garlic salt, pinch dry minced parsley. Refrigerate tightly covered, several hours before serving. Serves 6 sensibly!

PICKLED BEETS Like Smorgasbord

1-lb can sliced beets, undrained
1/3 cup light vinegar
3 TB lemon juice
2/3 cup sugar
1 TB tiny, hot, red cinnamon candies
2 sticks cinnamon (each about 2" long)
¼-tsp powdered cloves

Put everything into 1½-qt saucepan. Bring to boil, stirring often. Let boil briskly about 3 minutes. Remove from heat. Cover pan with a lid and let stand till mixture is cool. Refrigerate in covered container to serve within a month. Do NOT remove the cinnamon stick from this while storing this. Makes 4 salad bar servings.

Alternatives
Salad

SPAGHETTI-SHRIMP SALAD
Inspired by Bonanza's

Break the 8-oz strands of THIN spaghetti in half as you drop it into slightly salted, rapidly boiling water and cook till tender. One minute before cooking time is up add 8-oz frozen fully cooked shrimp to spaghetti. Let both drain while rinsing in colander under cold water, till cooled. Combine with 14-oz can sliced style stewed tomatoes, ½-cup Catalina Dressing, ¼-cup bottled Italian dressing, ¼-cup Sunflower Nuts, 1 cup minced celery & 3 or 4 spears of Chef Frank's Dill Pickles (see index) or Claussen Dills, diced fine, a pinch of dry parsley leaves & 1 tsp dry minced onion. Work in 1 cup of shredded Mozzarella & refrigerate the salad in tightly covered container 24 hrs before serving. Serves 4 to 6

Gloria Pitzer's MAKE ALIKE RECIPES

PARMESAN DRESSING —— STEAK HOUSE DRESSING
Inspired by Ponderosa Salad Bar

- 8-oz bottle Ranch Dressing
- 1 tsp black pepper
- 1/3 cup sour cream
- 1/3 cup grated Parmesan

Combine all ingredients as given. Keep refrigerated, tightly covered to use in a month. makes 1½-cups.

MC FABULOUS ORIENTAL DRESSING
Inspired by McDonald's

Favorite Recipe

- 7-oz jar babyfood strained apricots
- 3 TB Heinz 57 Sauce
- 3 TB bottled Italian Dressing
- 3 TB honey
- 3 TB sugar
- 3 TB soy sauce
- ½-cup bottled apple butter
- ½-cup Catalina dressing
- ½-cup ketchup

As listed mix all ingredients well, with wire whisk or electric mixer. Refrigerate tightly covered to use in 4 to 6 weeks. Do not freeze. Makes about a quart.

OLIVE GARDEN INSPIRED HOUSE DRESSING — JUST RIGHT.
A Wonderful Italian Dressing that will remind you of the famous Olive Garden Restaurant's house dressing.

- 1½-cups bottled Italian dressing
- 2 TB grated Parmesan cheese
- ? TB sugar (or Sweet & Low equal to that)
- 1 large raw egg (or Egg Beaters if necessary)

Hospitaliano! The Olive Garden

As listed put all 4 ingredients into blender. Blend high speed about a minute or till creamy looking. (It will appear transparent once you apply it to the salad.) Keep refrigerated, tightly capped to use in a week. (The raw egg used in this recipe works with the vinegar in the Italian dressing as if the egg had been cooked. It is used here just as we use it when making mayonnaise, so the egg takes on the composition of a fully cooked egg. But for those who are concerned, use Egg Beaters.) Makes just about a pint of dressing.

Greens consist of torn iceberg lettuce, Romain lettuce, fresh spinach leaves, finely shredded red cabbage used sparingly, plus diced tomatoes, peeled, sliced cukes & onions sliced into thin rings.

Lightly moisten greens in dressing & let stand 10 mins before adding other ingredients to salad & serve promptly.

Gloria Pitzer's Make Alike Recipes

FINE HERBS
1/4-cup each of dried parsley flakes, dried chervil leaves, dried minced chives, dried tarragon leaves, rubbed firmly through fine mesh sieve with back of spoon. Store out of direct sunlight to use in 6 months. Makes about 1 cup. Can be refrigerated up to a year.

CREAMY CAESAR DRESSING
Inspired by Red Lobster Restaurants

3/4-cup bottled Italian dressing	1/3 cup mayonnaise
1 TB grated Parmesan	1/2-tsp anchovie
1 TB sugar	paste or soy sauce

Use wire whisk to combine all ingredients as given. Keep refrigerated, tightly covered. Use in a week. Makes 12-oz

POPPYSEED DRESSING
Inspired by Marie Calender's Torrance, California

2/3 cup mayonnaise	3 TB white vinegar
1 cup Miracle Whip	2 tsp salt
4 TB sugar	1 tsp prepared mustard
3 TB light corn syrup	1 TB poppyseed

As given combine ingredients, using wire whisk till mixture is smooth. Refrigerate tightly capped to use within a month. Makes 1 pint. (Do not freeze, please!)

HONEY MUSTARD DRESSING Inspired by Chili's

1/3-cup mayonnaise	2 TB French's prepared mustard
1/3-cup Miracle Whip	1 TB Dijon mustard
1/4-cup honey	or more or less to taste

Combine all ingredients as listed using wire whisk till smooth. Refrigerate tightly covered to use in about 30 days. makes about a cupful. Do not freeze, please!

VINEGAR HOMEMADE Inspired by Heinz's
WINE VINEGAR is a good salad dressing ingredient, made by combining in non-metal 1-qt container, 1 cup cooking sherry or white wine (any kind or combination of wines) plus 1 cup white vinegar, 1 cup dark vinegar, 2 TB lemon juice, 12 whole cloves, 12 whole peppercorns, 1 peeled-clove garlic or 1/2-tsp garlic powder. Cover loosely, Let stand at room temperature 1 week, stirring occasionally & then strain, discarding food pieces. Refrigerate & use within 1 year. Makes about 3 1/2-cups.

Gloria Pitzer's MAKE ALIKE RECIPES

Pour It On Thick.
PICANTE SAUCE (Smooth Salsa)

14½-oz can stewed tomatoes - sliced style
8-oz can tomato sauce
1.5-oz pkg onion soup mix
1/4 cup bottled Italian Dressing

For "hot" salsa add the following:

1/2-tsp Tabasco Sauce
2 TB diced Jalepeno peppers
Dash Cayenne Pepper

incredible flavor—

SUPER

Put all ingredients into blender as listed & blend on high speed, till smooth. Keep refrigerated in covered container to use warmed or cold — within 3 weeks. Makes 3 cups.

Classic Blend
BARBECUE SAUCE
Inspired by Kraft's

8-oz bottle Kraft's creamy French Dressing
½-cup honey
¼-cup Heinz 57 Sauce
¼-cup ketchup

Mix all ingredients together well & use this to baste chicken, beef or pork as you would use any BBQ sauce..... per your favorite means of preparation. Makes 2 cups sauce.

Versatility
BARBECUE SAUCE
Inspired by Steak & Shake

8-oz A-1 Steak Sauce
8-oz Ketchup
16-oz Coca Cola

Mix all 3 ingredients together well. Makes 1-Qt. Keep refrigerated, well-covered, to use in 90 days.

Best Kept Secret

Everyone who likes to eat, and eat well, will enjoy the unique, delicious flavor of Durkee's Famous Sauce. Serve it with poultry, meats and seafood—as a seasoning for salad dressings, casseroles and sandwiches.

At home—or when dining out—enhance the flavor of your favorite foods with Durkee's Famous—America's best-loved sauce for almost 100 years.

One of Durkee's Famous Foods

DURKEE'S FAMOUS
SAUCE

—a unique product that can be used as a salad dressing all by itself, as an addition to mayonnaise or other dressings & as a good sandwich spread - but at the time of this writing it is $1.89 per 10-oz bottle...too much now...

FAMOUS SAUCE IMITATION
½-c cold water
4 TB cornstarch
½-cup plus 2 TB dark vinegar
2 TB salt (sounds like a lot but it is necessary to the final success of this product)

½-cup sugar (or artificial sweetener = to it)
1 whole egg
4 TB French's prepared mustard
4 TB margarine in tiny bits

Place all ingredients as listed in blender on high speed till smooth (2 minutes). Transfer to top of double boiler & cook over gently boiling water, stirring often for 12-15 mins or till thickened & smooth. Once more put mixture back through blender 30 seconds or till smooth, using high speed. Refrigerate in covered container 24 hrs before using. Makes 16-oz. Keeps refrigerated 3 months.

Gloria Pitzer's MAKE ALIKE RECIPES

HONEY MUSTARD SAUCE (Served with sandwiches or chicken)
Inspired by The Voyageur's of St. Clair, Michigan

Mix together 1/4-cup Dijon mustard, 1/2-cup Miracle Whip, 2 TB honey. Keep covered & refrigerated to use within 30 days. Makes about a cupful.

All Purpose Salad Dressing

Most restaurants offer the usual dressings for salads, and most are quite rich or not exactly what you are looking for. I've learned to make my own dressing from a few common ingredients that you can ask for without much trouble to the waitress or waiter. I mix together in a saucer, if nothing else, or even a small dish, by request or one I can find at the salad bar, about 1/4-cup (4 TB) vinegar, just as much water & just as much ketchup, plus 2 packets Sweet & Low or sugar to taste. This is usually sufficient for a one-serving size dinner salad or small Julienne Salad. Try it! You may think of something else to add to give it personality!

Fat-free

Restaurant

CAESAR DRESSING
Inspired by Red Lobster's - also like the Alibi Inn's

1/4-cup mayonnaise (not salad dressing)
1/4-cup bottled Ranch Dressing (Hidden Valley preferred)
1/4-cup Wish Bone Italian Dressing
1 TB white vinegar
1 TB water

Versatile

As listed combine all ingredients with wire whisk till perfectly smooth & creamy.

GREEK DRESSING: Add to above ingredients 1/4-tsp cumin powder, whisking it in well.

FOR CREAMY CAESAR DRESSING: To above ingredients whisk in 1 tsp anchovie paste or 1 TB soy sauce and 2 TB sour cream. Then refrigerate dressing tightly covered to use in 30 days. Do not freeze, please. Makes about a cupful.

CHEF FRANK'S VOYAGEUR DILL PICKLES
In 1/2-gallon plastic or glass container combine 5 medium cucumbers, peeled & sliced lengthwise in half & each half cut into 3 spears with 1 onion about the size of a lemon, quartered, 1 cup tarragon wine vinegar, 1-qt water, 1/4-cup sugar, or 12 packets Sweet & Low, 2 TB dry dill weed, 2 TB salt. cover tightly. Refrigerate 24 hrs before serving. Keep refrigerated to use in 2 weeks. Do not freeze please.

Gloria Pitzer's MAKE ALIKE RECIPES

THREE-IN-ONE SALAD DRESSING

Inspired by Farmer Jack's this basic dressing can be used on potato salad, macaroni salad & coleslaw, by adding only 1 other ingredient to the dressing for each salad & side-by-side on the same table, nobody would guess it was from the same basic dressing.

Mix together equal parts Miracle Whip, real mayonnaise & sour cream. For the **potato salad** add 1 TB French's prepared mustard to 1 cup of dressing. For **Macaroni Salad** add 1 TB sweet pickle relish to 1 cup dressing. For **Coleslaw** add 1 TB vinegar to 1 cup dressing, using enough dressing on each salad mixture just to moisten but not make "soupy"!

CREAMY GARLIC DRESSING
Inspired By Beef Carver Restaurant's

- 1½-cups mayonnaise
- ½-cup milk
- ¼-tsp Tabasco Sauce
- 1 tsp garlic salt
- 1 tsp prepared mustard
- 1 tsp dry minced oregano
- ¼-tsp black pepper
- ¼-tsp Dijon mustard

In order listed combine all ingredients using wire whisk to combine. Refrigerate, tightly covered, to use in a month. Do not freeze, please.

Ranch Dressing Mix
Inspired by Hidden Valley's

Lot for a Little.

Put 15 square 2" Saltine crackers through blender high speed till powdered. Add 1 cup dry minced parsley flakes, ½-cup dry minced onions, 2 TB dry dill weed. Blend again till powdered. Dump into bowl. Stir in ¼-cup each: onion salt, garlic salt, onion powder, garlic powder. funnel into container with tight-fitting lid. Store at room temp to use in 1 year. Makes 42-TB mix. 1 1 TB mix = 0.4-oz pkg store mix. TO USE MIX: Combine 1 TB mix, 1 cup mayo, 1 cup buttermilk. Makes 1 pint.

POTATO SALAD From Instant Mashed Potatoes

Combine 2½-cups each boiling water 7 boxed Instant Potato-Buds (Betty Crocker's), ½-cup milk, 1 cup small curd cottage cheese, ½-tsp salt, 1 tsp each: dry minced parsley, dry minced onion, plua 2 TB each: blender minced carrot(*) Blender minced celery & diced sweet pickle. work in 1/3-c Miracle Whip or less to taste. Refrigerate covered tightly 3 to 4 hrs before serving. Serves 4 to 6 sensibly.

Gloria Pitzer's MAKE ALIKE REICPES

SALADS

MARZESTY SLAW DRESSING

- 3 TB light vinegar
- 2 tsp salt
- 1 tsp prepared mustard
- 2/3 cup mayonnaise
- 1 cup Miracle Whip
- 4 TB sugar
- 3 TB light corn syrup

Beat all ingredients together well, just as listed, medium sized bowl, using a sturdy mixing spoon — rather than a mixer. Store in covered container and refrigerate to use within a month. Makes 1 pint.

NO YOLK MAYONNAISE

- 2 large egg whites
- Pinch salt (optional)
- 1 TB lemon juice
- 1 tsp Dijon mustard
- Dash Black Pepper
- 1 tsp cider vinegar
- 1 packet Sweet & Low or 1 tsp sugar
- 3/4-cup vegetable oil

In blender using slow speed, combine all BUT the oil. While motor is running on low, add oil in slow, thin, steady stream. Mayo will begin to thicken before the last 25% of it has been added, at which time you can hit the fast speed button on the blender just a few seconds, long enough to blend it all together quickly. Turn off motor. Transfer mixture to a refrigerator container with tight fitting lid. Refrigerate to be used within 10 days. Freeze to thaw and use within 6 months. Makes 1 cupful.

Salad Dressings

GOOD REASONS ITALIAN DRESSING MIX

- 1 TB garlic salt
- 1 TB onion powder
- 1 TB sugar
- 2 TB dry oregano leaves
- 1 tsp black pepper
- 1/4-tsp dry thyme
- 1 tsp dry Basil
- 1 TB parsley flakes
- 1/8-tsp dry mustard
- 1 envelope Lipton Cup A Soup Cream of Chicken powder OR
- 2 square soda crackers well- crushed + 1½-tsp chicken bouillon powder + 1 tsp non-dairy creamer powder
- 1/4-tsp celery salt
- 2 TB season salt (or Mrs. Dash)
- 1 TB bottled grated lemon rind

As given mix all ingredients together & force through fine mesh sieve with back of large spoon. Store in covered container to use in 4 to 5 months. Makes 1½-cups dry mix.------
TO USE THE MIX: Combine 2 TB of mix with 1/4-cup vinegar, 2/3 cup oil, 2 TB water. Shake mixture vigorously in tightly-capped container before applying to salad greens. (1 cupful)

Italian   **GOOD REASONS**

FOGCUTTER SALAD DRESSING

- ½-cup Mayonnaise
- ½-cup Miracle Whip
- 1 TB Dijon - Grey Poupon Mustard
- ¼-cup buttermilk
- 1 tsp onion salt

Mix it all together briskly with wire whisk. Store in covered container, refrigerated, to be used within 2 weeks. Makes about 1¼-cups.

Gloria Pitzer's MAKE ALIKE RECIPES

TUNA TWIX MIX Inspired by Nabisco's (1980)

Nabisco made a very good dry mix that you used with canned tuna and a few other ingredients. I was so impressed with the flavor and texture, it was a disappointment to find it no longer available in our area. To imitate it at home, here is what I do:

1 cup Rice Chex cereal or Corn Chex
  or use Bugles Corn Crackers

1 TB onion powder
1 TB dry minced onion
1 TB bottled grated lemon peel
1 envelope (0.4-oz) Ranch Dressing Mix (or see Index for homemade)
  (Use the pkg that prepares it with buttermilk)

As listed put all ingredients through blender till almost powdered, using high speed, on/off. Dump mixture into small bowl & stir in:

  1 TB dry minced parsley flakes
  2 TB canned dehydrated celery flakes

Store mixture in covered container on cupboard shelf to use within 6 to 8 weeks — out of direct sunlight & away from steam or heat.

TO USE THE MIX:

In small mixing bowl combine 4 TB of above mix with ¼-cup cold water. Add 6½-oz can drained, flaked tuna (preferably packed in spring water). Stir in ½-cup mayonnaise, 2 TB sweet pickle relish and 1 rib celery diced fine. Cover mixture & refrigerate for 1 hour before using as a sandwich spread. Makes 4 normal sandwiches — or one Mr. T type sandwich! (The Mix yields 8 TB).

GLORIFIED RICE Inspired by Sveden House

Bring 2 cups cranberry juice to boil. Add 2 cups Minute Rice. Cover. Remove from heat. Let stand 10 mins. Stir in 8-oz can DRAINED crushed pineapple, 2 cups miniature marshmallows. Cool completely. Fold in 1 pint heavy cream whipped stiff with 2 TB sugar or use 9-oz thawed Cool Whip. Refrigerate covered 24 hrs before serving. Serves 4 to 6. Do not freeze please!

TOMATO & SPICE DRESSING Inspired by Big Boy's

Combine ½-cup Miracle Whip salad dressing, 2 TB ketchup & 1 TB each Heinz 57 Sauce & light Karo corn syrup. Stir it with rubber bowl scraper till thoroughly blended. Makes about 3/4-cup dressing. Keep refrigerated. Do not freeze. Recipe may be doubled. (Keeps refrigerated to use within 30 days.)

RICE CONFETTI DELI SALAD like Farmer Jack's

Mix together 2 cups cold cooked rice, 2 cups miniature marshmallows, 1-lb can drained fruit cocktail, 1 cup chopped pecans, 10-oz jar drained red Maraschino cherries sliced, 1 cup flaked coconut, 9-oz container thawed Cool Whip & 1 cup sour cream. Refrigerate in covered container 24 hrs before serving. Serves 6-8

you can't tell the difference

Gloria Pitzer's MAKE ALIKE RECIPES

Specialty Sauces

HAMBURGER SAUCE
Inspired by Goody Goody's (Dayton, Ohio 1970's)

12-oz bottle Heinz Chili Sauce
½-cup sweet pickle relish
¼-cup Ketchup
1 TB dry minced onion
1 TB sugar
4 TB mayonnaise
¼-tsp garlic salt
Dash black pepper

Mix all ingredients together well. Refrigerate, covered, to use within 30 days. Makes about 2½-cups sauce. (Do not freeze!)

SWEET & SOUR SAUCE — *If you like Kraft's, you'll like this one!*

8-oz can chunk pineapple, undrained
¼-cup orange juice
2/3 cup packed brown sugar
1 TB dehydrated bell pepper flakes
2 TB cornstarch
½-cup cider vinegar
¼-tsp paprika
½-tsp season salt

As listed put all ingredients into blender. Blend till smooth on high speed, about ½-minute. Pour into 2-qt saucepan. Cook, stirring constantly on med-heat, using wire whisk till smooth & thickened. Remove from heat. Refrigerate, covered, 1 hour before using. (1 pint).

HARDLY'S MUSHROOM SAUCE
(Inspired by Hardee's Restaurant sauce for hamburgers)

Into blender put 14-oz can clear beef broth, 1 cup prepared black tea, cold - and 1 tsp season salt, ½-cup Bisquick. Blend ½-minute high speed till smooth. Pour into saucepan. Cook on med-high, stirring constantly till thick & smooth. Remove at once from heat. Stir in 1-lb fresh, sliced, sauteed mushrooms. Spoon over hamburger patty on sliced bun, before adding top half of bun. For 4

SEASONING MIX for French Fries & other foods
Inspired by Rally's (1991)

¼-tsp dry mustard
¼-tsp ground ginger
½-tsp black pepper
2 TB season salt

Combine well & use as a seasoning on fried food soon as you remove from hot oil. Apply to food according to taste and store at room temperature to use in 1 yr.

COAST TO COAST
Honey-Mustard Sauce   McFABULOUS! For Chicken Nuggets

¼-cup honey
2 TB French's prepared mustard
1 TB Heinz 57 Sauce

Spray your measuring cup with Pam before measuring your honey and it will slip right out of the cup. Stir the honey together with the mustard and 57 Sauce. Store in small covered container to use within 2 weeks. Makes about ½-cupful.

Gloria Pitzer's MAKE ALIKE RECIPES

JUST RIGHT

TARTAR SAUCE
Inspired by The Red Lobster's

Combine in small bowl: ½-cup Kraft's real mayonnaise, ¼-cup sweet pickle relish, 2 TB Miracle Whip salad dressing, 1 TB sugar, ½-tsp dry minced parsley, ¼-tsp onion powder. (1 cup)

SAUCES FOR VEGETABLES
Originally put out by Bird's Eye
(No longer available...)

New England Style

2 TB margarine, melted
1 tsp light corn syrup
½-tsp onion salt
½-tsp onion powder
½-tsp dry minced parsley
1 tsp grated Parmesan cheese

2 TB water
1/3 cup cooked, drained seashell macaroni
½-cup frozen uncooked, unthawed broccoli cuts
½-cup frozen French style green beans
½-cup frozen whole kernel corn
1 TB chopped sweet red pepper or ripe tomato without seeds

Place the ingredients, just as listed in 1½-qt saucepan, stirring over medium heat till it comes to a boil. Boil gently about 4 to 6 minutes, or till vegetables become limp. Remove from heat. Cover and let stand 8 or 10 minutes and then return to medium heat, bringing just to a boil till vegetables are tender. Serve undrained with ½-cup of unseasoned croutons sprinkled over top of vegetables. Serves 4.

Japanese Style

2 TB margarine, melted
1 tsp light corn syrup
1 tsp chicken bouillion powder
½-tsp onion powder
1/8 tsp turmeric

½-cup pearl onions—frozen & unthawed
½-cup French style green beans
½-cup broccoli cuts
½-cup sliced canned, drained mushrooms
2 TB chopped sweet red pepper or ripe tomatoes without seeds
¼-cup water

FRESH TO PREPARE ON THE SPOT – These sauce recipes are OUTSTANDING!

Cook 'n' Serve

Place all ingredients as listed in 1½-qt saucepan, stirring over medium heat till comes to boil. Boil gently 4 to 6 mins or till vegetables are limp. Remove from heat. Cover & let stand 8 or 10 mins and then return to medium heat, bringing just to boil till vegetables are tender. Serve undrained at once. Serves 4.

Sumptuous Sauces

Gloria Pitzer's MAKE ALIKE RECIPES

BBQ sauce - Texas Style

Easy

½-cup A-1 Steak Sauce
½-cup Ketchup
½-cup Heinz 57 Sauce
¼-cup Worcestershire Sauce
8-oz Coca Cola (Diet or regular)

Add a pinch of dry mustard for extra hot!

Combine all ingredients as listed. Refrigerate tightly covered to use within 30 days. Makes almost 3 cups.

BEARNAISE SAUCE

Mix together 1 cup prepared Hollandaise sauce, 1 TB vinegar & 1 TB dry minced onions, gently heated and used with poultry. Makes about 1¼-cups.

Hollandaise - PDQ

In 1½-qt saucepan using wire whisk, combine 1 cup mayonnaise (not salad dressing), 2 eggs, 3 TB lemon juice, ½-tsp dry mustard. On medium heat, whisk till smooth & thickened but don't let it boil! Keep it piping hot. remove from heat soon as it resembles smooth pudding. Serve promptly on asparagus or fish.

HONEY MUSTARD DRESSING Inspired by Chili's

Combine ½-cup Miracle Whip, ¼-cup mayonnaise, ¼-cup honey and 2 TB Dijon mustard (Grey Poupon), plus 1 tsp prepared yellow mustard. Makes about 1½-cups. Keep refrigerated, covered.

This was a good first step.

SALAD SUPREME SEASONING MIX is a product made by McCormick Spices. It is the main ingredient in popular pasta salads. If you cannot find the product where you shop, you can recreate a Make-Alike version this way:

SUPER SALAD SEASONING MIX:

2 TB sesame seeds
1 TB season salt
1 TB paprika
½-tsp black pepper
2 packets Herb Ox chicken broth powder or bouillon powder
3 TB grated Parmesan
1 TB poppy seeds
1 tsp onion salt
¼-tsp garlic powder
1 envelope Tomato-Cup of Soup powder (by Campbell or Lipton)

As given, mix all ingredients together & funnel into jar with tight-fitting cap. Store at room temp. Use in 90 days Makes 1 cup seasonong. (Tomato Cup Soup Make-Alike given in our Best of Better Cookery Cookbook.)

Gloria Pitzer's MAKE ALIKE RECIPES

SMOKED SALMON — THOROUGHLY MODERN

SMOKING FISH AT HOME

- 1-qt warm water (95F-)
- ½-cup canning salt or Kosher salt
- 1/3 cup sugar
- 3 TB pure maple syrup
- 2 TB soy sauce
- 1 clove garlic minced
- ¼-tsp black pepper
- ¼-tsp Tabasco Sauce
- 4 to 5-lbs salmon fillets each about 1" thick
- 2 cups hickory chips

Combine all but hickory chips in large enameled or stainless steel bowl (NOT aluminum). Mix till salt is dissolved. Add a plate to top of mixture with a weight on it to keep fish submerged in the brine. Marinate in refrigerator 8 hrs or overnight. Turn pieces occasionally. Remove salmon from marinade. Discard marinade. Rinse fillets. Pat dry. Place salmon on racks, flesh side up. Let dry at room temperature until surface is slight sticky (about an hour). Meanwhile, soak hickory chips in cold water just to cover, for 30 mins. Drain chips. Wrap in heavy aluminum foil. Leave 1 end open to allow smoke to escape. Place package on "coals" of an electric or gas barbeque out-of-doors. Close barbecue lid. Turn heat to medium. When chips begin to smoke, (5 mins), reduce heat to lowest possible temp. Arrange salmon in single layer on 2 sheets foil, fashioned into a pan or use disposable foil pan. Set this on barbecue. Close lid & let smoke until meat thermometer inserted into salmon registers 140F-, about an hour. Cool fillets. Wrap & refrigerate till chilled. Keeps well for 1 week refrigerated.

NOTE: Salmon can also be smoked on a standard charcoal barbecue. Sprinkle soaked and drained hickory chips over hot coals. Grill salmon until flesh turns opaque, turning pieces once. Or use a home smoker, smoking salmon 4 to 5 hrs at 95F-.

Sour Cream HOMEMADE like Grandma did!

2 cups heavy cream and 5 teaspoons buttermilk. Put these two ingredients in a screw-type jar and shake one minute. Let stand at room temperature 48 hours. The mixture will thicken. Refrigerate at least 24 hours before using.

Gloria Pitzer's MAKE ALIKE RECIPES

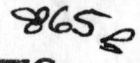

POPULAR PRODUCTS

MAKING SWEET PICKLES OUT OF DILL PICKLES

1-quart jar store-bought Kosher dill pickles
1-lb box brown sugar (light preferred)
1 TB mixed pickling spices
½-cup white vinegar

Drain & reserve juice from pickles in 2-qt saucepan. Set aside. Slice pickles ¼" thick & set these aside. To the pickle juice in the pan add sugar & spices & bring to boil. Set timer to let it boil gently 10 mins. Strain boiling liquid into another 2-qt pan, discarding spices. Add vinegar to hot liquid & stir in pickle slices. Allow to stand uncovered 1 hr. Pack then into refrigerator container with tight fitting lid. Refrigerate to use within 90 days. Freeze to thaw & use in 6 months.

SUGAR-FREE SWEET PICKLES Customized

Follow recipe above for regular sweet pickles, but substitute artificial "Brown Sugar Twin" equal to amount of sugar. Use only what the box prescribes will be equal to 1-lb of real sugar, continuing as recipe directs.

SIMMERING POTPOURRI

Make your own delightful fragrances to ward-off the offensive, lingering odors of foods & stuffy rooms.

BEGIN WITH a small skillet or saucepan. In it combine 2 cups water, 2 TB cinnamon, 1 TB apple pie spice, 1 TB ground allspice, about a tspful ground cloves. Let it simmer gently on back burner of your stove about 10 mins, replacing water as needed if it evaporates. You can allow mixture to stand in pan uncovered, to be returned to the stove as you feel it's needed. OR use this in an electric simmering potpourri "Crock Pot". Devise your own by using a Mr. Coffee Pyrex coffeepot containing the potpourri mixture, keeping it on the Mr. Coffee heating-unit. Throw in some fresh orange peels or lemon peels now & then to enhance the fragrance. You can let the mixture stand at room temperature when not being heated, and reuse it over and over again, adding new spices and water to the old mixture to revitalize it.---

Gloria Pitzer's MAKE ALIKE RECIPES

VANILLA EXTRACT HOMEMADE

You can buy vanilla beans wherever spices are sold. Spice Island brand is in a bottle. Split 4 vanilla beans & bury them in ¼-cup sugar in a jar. Cover tightly. Let stand 1 week at room temperature. Then put the beans & the sugar into small saucepan. Add ½-cup water. Bring to boil. Boil rapidly 2 mins. Stir constantly. Remove from heat. Cool & put through blender to puree. Cap tightly again and let stand 1 week again. Strain mixture through coffee filter lined strainer, reserving the strained liquid. Add to that 4-oz vodka. Keep at room temperature indefinitely in tightly capped bottle or jar. Use exactly as you would store-shelf vanilla extract, which, by the way, is usually 35% alcohol by volume, which is the reason vodka is used in the homemade version.

Products for diverse needs

VELVET CHEESE SPREAD Inspired by Velveeta

Requested over & over since we sold out our Jan-Feb '90 issue in which this recipe 1st appeared!

12-oz pkg American Cheese slices ("Singles")
8-oz jar Cheez Whiz
8-oz pkg cream cheese
4-oz pkg chredded sharp Cheddar

As lsited, put all into top of double boiler over simmering water, stirring often till melted & smooth & then switch to electric mixer to beat to combine. Pour into pam-sprayed margarine tubs or freezer containers with tight-fitting lids. Refrigerate 12 to 15 hrs before using OR freeze to thaw & use within a 6 month period. Makes 2-lbs at about $2.25 per lb.

CHEESE WISH Smooth Cheese Product Inspired by Cheez Whiz

Into blender put 2 cups milk, 1/3 cup cornstarch, 1 tsp season salt, ½-tsp paprika. Blend till smooth high speed. Pour into heavy saucepan & cook, stirring constantly over med-heat, till thickened and smooth like a pudding. (*Watch it! It may scorch if heat is too high!*) Remove from heat at 1st few bubbles of a boil and stir in 16 slices (Singles) American Cheese each torn into bits, stirring till completely melted & perfectly smooth. Using portable electric mixer, beat 1 to 2 mins. Beat in 4 TB butter or margarine. Pour into container with tight fitting lid. Refrigerate to use within 30 days or freeze to thaw & use within 6 month period. Makes 3½ to 4 cups.

KETCHUP Inspired by Brook's - 1950's

No canning involved. It freezes beautifully to use in a year, or keeps refrigerated to use in 90 days.

- 14-oz can stewed tomatoes
- 6-oz cider vinegar
- 1 TB season salt
- ½-tsp cinnamon
- 2 TB cornstarch
- 6-oz can tomato paste
- 1 tsp dry mustard
- 3/4-cup firmly packed light brown sugar
- 2 tsp onion powder
- ¼-tsp ground nutmeg
- ¼-tsp ground cloves
- 2 TB butter or margarine
- ½-tsp Tabasco Sauce

As listed, put all ingredients into blender & blend high speed till smooth, turning motor off periodically to clean mixture away from blades & to scrape down sides of container. Resume blending till smooth. Pour into 2½-qt saucepan & cook, stirring constantly over med-high till comes just to boil. **Immediately** remove from heat before it scorches. Let cool to lukewarm, funnel into quart container with tight-fitting lid. Keep refrigerated to use in 90 days. Freeze to use within a year. Makes 1-Qt.

STRAWBERRY JAM (Without Pectin)

STRAWBERRIES grew wild in the back of our property in Pearl Beach when our 5 children were youngsters. These plants were remnants of the farm that was once there surrounding the then-80-year-old house. I made jam every spring as soon as the June berries were ripe. I used my mother's recipe. Only 4 ingredients!

- 6 cups whole, ripe strawberries with hulls removed
- 2 cups sifted powdered sugar
- 4 cups granulated sugar
- 1/3 cup lemon juice bottled or fresh

Wash berries well & drain. Layer berries with sugar in kettle or Dutch oven. Let stand at room temp 4 hours. Bring then to a boil over low heat, stirring carefully & often until sugar dissolves. Add lemon juice. Boil briskly, stirring constantly, shaking kettle occasional to help settle berries, for 10 mins or till berries are plump and the syrup is thick & translucent. Pour into shallow pan & skim. Let stand, shaking pan occasionally, till cold (shaking helps berries absorb syrup & keeps them plump). Pour into hot sterilized jelly glasses. Seal at once with thin layer of melted paraffin. Makes 4 half-pints.

Gloria Pitzer's MAKE ALIKE RECIPES

SUGAR-FREE KETCHUP - NO CANNING REQUIRED!!!

This should be an inspiration to others as there are no sugar-free ketchups on the market at this time.... Make this up in small amounts or double it & freeze it!

- 6-oz tomato paste
- ¼-cup oil
- ¼-cup margarine (soft)
- 2 packets Sweet & Low
- 2 TB vinegar
- 5 TB chicken bouillon powder

Combine all ingredients in 1-qt mixing bowl 7 using electric mixer, beat till smooth. Refrigerate tightly covered to use within 8 weeks. Makes 1¼-cups ketchup. Recipe may be doubled. It freezes well to thaw & use within 6 months. (1¼-cups = 20 TB of which 6 TB are fat.)

CHICKEN BROTH CONCENTRATE
Inspired by The Garden Restaurant - Tulsa, Oklahoma

Served in little demi-cups this rich clear broth is unique. Heat together 25-oz can clear chicken broth, 12-oz water, 2 boneless, skinless chicken breasts in small pieces. Bring to boil. Simmer gently uncovered till chicken meat is milky white, thoroughly done. Remove chicken from broth with slotted spoon. Cover & refrigerate chicken to use later in salads. To the broth on low heat, add 2 packets Herb-Ox chicken broth powder or 3 tsp chicken bouillon powder plus 1 beaten egg AND shell, which clarifies broth. Allow to simmer few mins till egg & shell rise to top, making broth below crystal clear. Strain broth through fine mesh sieve. Refrigerate broth tightly covered to reheat & serve piping hot in small cups within a few days or freeze to thaw & heat within 4 months. makes 4 to 6 small servings.

STEWED TOMATOES - Freezer Style
Inspired by Del Monte's

Drop 15 lg ripe tomatoes briefly into boiling water & then briefly into ice water to loosen skins so they can be easily peeled. Slice tomatoes & dop into 4-qt saucepan. Dust in 2 TB salt & cook, medium heat, stirring just till juices form. Turn heat to low. Add 2 large, seeded, green peppers, diced, 1 white onion the size of an orange, diced fine and 6 ribs celery sliced thin. Cover 7 cook on lowest heat till vegetables are tender. Stir occasionally. Adjust seasoning to taste with season salt, pepper, and sugar to taste if desired. Cool to lukewarm. Divide between freezer containers, with tight flutting lids. Leave 1" head space. Seal lids in masking tape. Freeze to use within 6 months.

Gloria Pitzer's MAKE ALIKE RECIPES

LOOKING BACK

ONION SOUP Inspired by Win Schuler's (Michigan)

If you remember Win Schuler's very good onion soup from his Marshall, Michigan restaurant, you may like this unusual imitation.

- 10-oz can Franco American Beef Gravy
- 10-oz can Campbell's Beef Broth
- 2 TB butter or margarine
- ¼-cup dry chopped onion
- 2 (½" thick each) slices French Bread
- 4 TB grated Parmesan cheese
- 4 TB mayonnaise
- ½-cup Sweet Vermouth

Schuler's — Combine first 4 ingredients in Teflon lined 2-qt saucepan over med-high heat, just till piping hot and onion flakes are tender. Do not let it boil. (About 10 minutes). Cut slices of bread in pieces to fit top of oven broof soup bowls. Ladle soup into 4 oven-proof soup bowls. Combine Parmesan with mayonnaise to make a paste. Divide between 4 pieces of French Bread. Float these pieces of bread atop each of the servings of soup and place them 4" from broiler heat, just for half a minute or so to let cheese mixture bubble and turn golden. Serve at once. Makes 4 servings.

Soup

Worth waiting for.
BOSTON (New England) CREAMY CLAM CHOWDER

This is a smooth, potato-y clam chowder that should have started with diced salt-pork, but instead has the illusion of having been made that way with the subtle addition of a few drops of liquid hickory flavoring, "liquid smoke". My husband, Paul, thinks this is a good, smooth clam chowder, but he likes the revised version of Howard Johnson's best.

- 10-oz can clear chicken broth
- 3 TB cornstarch
- 3 TB non-dairy creamer powder
- 1 TB dry minced onion
- 3 cans (6½-oz each) undrained clams
- 10-oz can cream of celery soup
- ½-tsp dry minced parsley leaves
- ½-tsp onion POWDER (not salt!)
- Dash black pepper —or to taste
- ¼-scant- tsp liquid smoke (optional)
- Pinch dry Thyme leaves (optional)
- 3 medium baked potatoes peeled & crumbled (2 cups approx)

Put 1st 3 ingredients through blender on high speed just till smooth. Pour mixture into 2½-qt saucepan, stirring constantly while cooking over med-high, just till smooth & thickened. Add remaining ingredients, as listed, stirring well just to combine. Never let the mixture boil! Serve when piping hot. Serves 6 nicely. Do not freeze, but you may refrigerate leftovers tightly covered to rewarm in 3 or 4 days.

PEANUT SOUP Rich & Creamy

- 10-oz can cream celery soup
- 10-oz can cream chicken soup
- Half of soup can milk
- 1/3 cup peanut butter
- 1/3 cup dry roasted peanuts, chopped
- ½-tsp dry minced onion
- Pinch dry parsley flakes

In top of double boiler ov- simmering water, combine all ingredients, stirring to blend well. When piping hot, serve promptly with a dalop of sour cream atop each serving & capsule- shaped cheese crackers, a few floating on top of each of 4 to 6 servings. Do not let soup boil! Do not freeze.

Gloria Pitzer's MAKE ALIKE RECIPES

SWISS ONION SOUP
Inspired by Fogcutter (Pt. Huron, Mich)

In 2-qt saucepan combine 14-oz can clear chicken broth and a 10-oz. can clear beef broth with 1 TB dry minced onion, 1 tsp onion powder. Bring just to a boil. At once remove from heat and stir in ½-cup Sweet Vermouth. Divide between 4 oven-proof soup bowls and float a thin slice of Party Rye bread atop each serving. Place 2 TB shredded Swiss cheese on bread & put bowls 4" from broiler heat for half a minute or till cheese bubbles. Serve at once. Serves 4.

authentic Italian
PASTA FAGIOLI (Or Pasta Fazula)
Inspired by The Olive Garden's

- 1-lb can undrained Northern beans
- 2 cans (14-oz each) sliced style stewed tomatoes
- 2 cans (14-oz each) clear beef broth
- 1-lb jar Prego spaghetti sauce
- 2 ribs celery thinly sliced
- 1 onion the size of a lemon, chopped
- 2 cups small spiral pasta uncooked
- Salt & pepper to taste

Combine everything in Dutch oven on med-high heat. Bring just to boil. Turn to low. Cover pan with lid. Allow to cook gently 30 mins or till pasta is tender. Serves 6 - 8

VEGETABLE BEEF SOUP
Inspired by Bob Evans Restaurants (1989)
EASY-ON-THE-BUDGET
Fast To Prepare

- ¾-to-1-lb ground round
- 4 TB oil
- 1 envelope onion soup mix
- 1 envelope mushroom-onion soup mix
- 7 cups (40-oz can) clear chicken broth
- 1-lb bag frozen soup vegetables
- 1-lb can undrained sliced potatoes
- 8-oz can (small size) stewed tomatoes, cut up
- 10-oz can beef gravy
- ½-cup blender-minced celery(*)

In Dutch oven or large soup kettle heat the oil on high & brown beef in this, crumbling with fork, till all pink color disappears. Turn heat to med-high. Add all remaining ingredients. Bring just to a boil. At once turn heat to gentle simmer. Put lid on kettle. Let simmer very gently 1 hour minimum, 3 hours maximum before serving. Freeze in tightly sealed containers to thaw & reheat within a 6 month period. Refrigerate (tightly covered) to reheat in a week's time. Makes 8 to 10 servings.

(*) Fill blender half full water. Add 2 to 3 ribs celery in 2" pieces. Blend high speed only few seconds till minced. Drain in strainer or freeze in blender water to use in 6 mos

Gloria Pitzer's MAKE ALIKE RECIPES

Vegetable Soup — Inspired by Jimmy Launce

No Fat – No Meat – No Salt & still delicious!

Inspired by Jimmy Launce's mouth-watering description of a homemade soup that this WJR-Radio-Detroit talk-show host prepares without a recipe yet! It's a super soup considering it has no fat, no meat, no-salt & is still wonderful & healthy. We added season salt to taste, however, because salt is not a problem for us. I took some shortcuts using V-8 Juice as the basis of my broth, where Jimmy uses fresh tomatoes to create his broth. I came up with a 2nd alternative while camping one chilly weekend, using pantry shelf canned ingredients. Take your choice!

GARDEN VEGETABLE SUPER SOUP

(Fresh, Frozen or Canned – 3 recipes)

- 24-oz V-8 Juice
- 2 cups water
- 1 cup minced celery
- 2 cups diced cabbage
- 1½-cups thin sliced potatoes
- 1 small onion diced fine
- 2 cups fresh diced mushrooms
- 1/3 cup fresh minced parsley
- Salt & pepper to taste
- 4 tomatoes peeled & diced
- 1 small green pepper diced
- either 2 cups fresh OR 10-oz pkg frozen of each
  - whole kernal corn
  - cut green beans
  - sliced carrots
- 1 tsp each: thyme leaves, coriander & cilantro

In Dutch oven – high heat, bring just to boil. Cover & reduce heat to simmer 20 mins or till vegetables are tender. Freeze in small portions to rewarm in 90 days. (2½-Qts).

VEGETABLE SOUP Camper's Pantry Shelf Style

- 24-oz V-8 Juice
- 2 cups water
- 1 cup minced celery
- 2 cups diced cabbage
- 3 TB ketchup (optional)
- 1 tsp each: thyme leaf, ground coriander and dry cilantro leaves
- Salt/Pepper to taste (optional)
- 1-lb can each undrained
  - mushrooms,
  - stewed tomatoes sliced
  - sliced carrots
  - cut green beans
  - sliced potatoes
- 1 tsp dry minced parsley
- 1 TB dry minced onion

NUTRITIOUS

In Dutch oven – high heat, bring just to boil. Cover & reduce heat to simmer just till cabbage is tender (8-10 mins) Serve piping hot. Freeze in small portions to use in about 90 days. Makes about 2½-qts.

NOTE: Other fresh vegetables of your choice can be used in place of those mentioned above, or in addition-to, providing then that you add more water if becomes too thick.

Ours doesn't have to take hours

Gloria Pitzer's MAKE ALIKE RECIPES

SUMMER SOUP Inspired by Bonanza's (1987)

Serve this thick soup cold with soy sauce like chop suey in hot weather or as a hearty winter hot sidedish.

In 2½-qt saucepan bring 5 cups water to brisk boil. Add 2 cups slightly broken ¼" wide egg noodles, 2 TB chicken bouillon powder, 1-lb can sliced carrots undrained & ½ cup minced celery, 1 tsp dry minced onion. Simmer till noodles are tender. Remove from heat. Stir in 1 cup dry Minute Rice. Cover with lid tightly. Let stand 15 mins. Refrigerate covered to serve within a week. Serves 4 to 6. Freezing not recommended.

CREAM OF BROCCOLI SOUP Inspired by Big Boy (1991)

(The earlier version with ham & mushrooms as it was served 6 or 8 yrs ago is in our FAST FOOD BOOK.)

In medium saucepan cook 10-oz pkg frozen chopped broccoli in enough slightly salted water to cover, med-high heat, till tender. Remove from heat. Drain. Reserve cooking water. Set broccoli aside. Add enough cold water to cooking water to equal 4 cups. Allow to cool. Put into blender along with 1 cup instant nonfat dry milk powder, 2/3 cup flour, 14-oz can clear chicken broth. Blend high speed few seconds till smooth. Pour into 2½-qt saucepan. Use wire whisk to cook, stirring constantly, over med-high till thickened & smooth. Do not let it boil or it may scorch. When slightly thickened, remove from heat. Add broccoli. Keep warm in top of double boiler over hot water up to an hour before serving. Serves 4 to 6. Refrigerate unused portions, tightly covered, to rewarm within a few days. Freeze to use within 4 months.

CHICKEN THIS EVENING SAUCE (Country French Style)
Inspired by Ragu's Special Sauce — **Cream Sauce**

Combine: 10-oz can cream chicken soup, 6-oz Wishbone bottled Ranch Dressing, ¼-c Kraft's Free Italian Dressing, ¼-cup Chablis wine (optional), 8-oz can sliced carrots drained & diced, plus liquid only from 8-oz can mushrooms. (Freeze mushrooms to use in 6 months), plus ½-tsp dry Thyme leaves. TO USE SAUCE: In lg skillet in 2 TB oil, brown 3-lbs chicken pieces 8 mins. Add sauce. Cover with lid. Simmer 30 mins to desired doneness. (3 cups sauce). Or oven brown in 9x13" pan, 375F- 15 mins. Add sauce. Seal in foil on 3 sides. Bake 45 mins-to-1 hr or till tender.

Gloria Pitzer's MAKE ALIKE RECIPES

DIRTY RICE Inspired by Popeye's (Cajun)

Brown 1-lb spicy bulk-style breakfast sausage in skillet, med-high heat till pink color disappears, crumbling with fork. Stir in 14-oz can clear chicken broth, ½-cup long grain rice, 1 tsp dry minced onion. Simmer gently covered, 18-20 mins or till rice is tender & most of broth is absorbed. Serve promptly to 4.

San Diego

THE HUDDLE RESTAURANT at 4023 Goldfinch St - San Diego, owned by Robert and Ruth Henricks, serve our Tomato Florentine Soup and they tell us their guests rave about it.

TOMATO FLORENTINE SOUP
(Inspired by Shoney's - Ohio-Missouri)

2 cans (14-oz each) clear chicken broth
14-oz can sliced style stewed tomatoes
12-oz V-8 Juice
10-oz can cream of tomato soup

1 TB sugar
10-oz box frozen chopped spinach
Dash nutmeg
Salt & pepper to taste

In large soup kettle or saucepan combine 1st 4 ingredients with wire whisk over medium heat. Add remaining ingredients, without even thawing the spinach. Allow to heat gently 30 mins on med-low or till spinach is tender. Keep hot without letting it boil. Serves 6 sensibly. Freeze leftovers to thaw and rewarm within 6 months.

DELICATESSEN Delicious NEW

DELI CABBAGE SOUP Using Sugar

10-oz can tomato soup
16-oz water
2 cans (1-lb ea) tomatoes, cut-up
1 onion the size of an egg, diced
HALF of a 1-lb head cabbage, diced
2 TB soy sauce
1 TB lemon juice
1/3-cupful packed, brown sugar

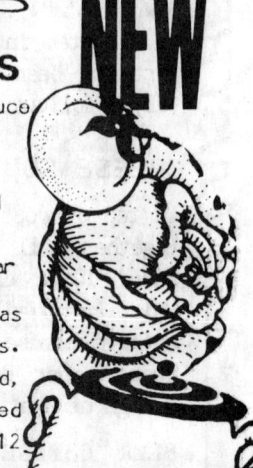

Combine in Dutch Oven, all ingredients as listed. Bring just to boil. Boil hard 2 mins. Transfer to 14-cup Slow Cooker & cook, covered, on HIGH 1 hour, on LOW 4 to 7 hours as needed till cabbage is quite tender & limp. makes 12 cup-sized or 8-bowl sized servings. Freezes well to use within 6 months.

BEAN SOUP Inspired by Bill Knapp's

Prepare this overnight in your slow cooker! The secret is not presoaking the beans, but baking them dry, first.

1-lb dry Northern beans	14-oz can clear chicken broth
2 qts water	½-tsp black pepper
1 envelope onion soup mix	½-tsp liquid smoke
3 smoked ham hocks OR use 1-lb ham steak in bits	14-oz can sliced style stewed tomatoes

In ungreased 9" pie pan bake dry beans uncovered at 375F- 20 mins. Combine beans with water, onion soup mix, ham hocks in slow cooker on high 4 hours, covered. Add everything else & cook on low 12 to 14 hrs (overnight) or till beans are tender, but not mushy. Freeze in small portions to thaw & reheat withing 4 months. Refrigerate to use in a week. Serves 8 adequately or 6 generously!

SPLIT PEA SOUP

Follow recipe above but instead of dry Northern beans, put 1-lb dry split peas in ungreased pie pan & bake uncovered as directed above. Continue as recipe above otherwise says.

LENTIL SOUP

Follow recipe above for bean soup, using 1-lb dry lentils instead of beans. Follow beans soup recipe exactly as it otherwise directs above.

BLACK EYED PEA SOUP
BLACK BEAN SOUP

As directed in recipe for Bean Soup above, use instead of Northern beans, either black eyed peas or black beans (dry), following bean soup recipe exactly.

CHEESE SOUP Inspired by Denny's

In top of double boiler over gently simmering water, stir together till smooth: **2 cans (10-oz each) cream celery soup, 10-oz can cream of chicken soup, 8-oz jar Cheez Whiz, ½-cup milk, 1 TB dry minced onion, ¼-cup small curd cottage cheese, ¼-cup real mayonnaise, dash or 2 of black pepper,** but do not add salt since Cheez Whiz contains enough of that. When piping hot serves 4 favorably!

BEER CHEESE SOUP: To above cheese soup recipe add 12-oz can beer or non-alcoholic beer as last ingredient. A dash of Tobasco is nice also!

Gloria Pitzer's MAKE ALIKE RECIPES

Soup From Scratch
Chicken Broth

Weary of finding MSG & other unwanted ingredients in canned soups, here is an alternative. The broth can be frozen in 14-oz containers to use in place of the 14-oz can of clear chicken broth called for in some of my recipes, using it within a 6 month period if properly wrapped.

This is more a "technique" than it is a recipe because the weight & size of ingredients will vary.

BEGIN WITH A DUTCH OVEN on the top of the stove. In this we'll put about 1-lb chicken necks, 1-lb chicken wings & 4 or 5 chicken breasts (with skin) into the kettle, covering that with just enough water that it comes 1" from rim of kettle. Bring to a brisk boil. Cover the pan & allow to simmer gently 1 hour or till meat falls from the bones and fat is very limp. Allow to cool to lukewarm. Use slotted spoon to remove chicken pieces from broth, dropping these pieces into a colander over another pan or bowl that will catch any dripping broth from the pieces. (We want to salvage every drop possible. Collect all of the strained and clear broth in Dutch Oven. Cover with lid. Refrigerate at least overnight till all fat comes to the top and becomes solid enough that you can lift it right out of the broth. Discarding all of the solid fat & the bones & pieces of the chicken, except the breast pieces that can be used in other recipes, pour the broth through a fine mesh strainer & return once more to top of stove, adding to it a big white onion (about the size of an orange), in pieces, 4 or 5 ribs celery with leaves in 3 inch pieces, 1 or 2 bay leaves, 1 tsp dry thyme leaves, 1 TB dry minced parsley & 4 or 5 carrots, peeled & grated on large whole of vegetable grater, or minced with water in blender & drained before adding to soup. Bring to brisk boil. Cover & turn down to simmer 1½ hrs or till vegetables are tender. Then strain again through fine mesh strainer. Discard all of vegetables & such. Season to taste with salt & pepper & pinch or so of sugar if you wish. Freeze in 14-oz cartons sealing lids twice in freezer tape. Date to use in 6 mos.
FOR BEEF BROTH—In place of chicken in above recipe, use beef neck bones, stewing beef & round steak and continue otherwise as recipe for chicken broth directs.

The Genuine Alternative.

Gloria Pitzer's MAKE ALIKE RECIPES

MARTY'S SALAD as served at The Buggy Works Restaurant, on the corner of Orchard Lake Road & 13 Mile in Franklin, Mich is unique and wonderful. After dozens of failures I finally came up with my version of their **Salad Dressing**

SWEET & SOUR SALAD DRESSING for a salad inspired by The Buggy Works

- 14-oz can Eagle Brand Milk
- 1 cup light Karo corn syrup
- 1/2-cup white vinegar
- 1 1/2-cups Miracle Whip
- 1/4-lb (1 stick) margarine sliced in small pieces

In top of double boiler over simmering water, combine all the above ingredients with a wire whisk until margarine is completely melted. Let cook over simmering water 30 mins (set timer) stirring occasionally. Put mixture through blender, using high speed few seconds, just to combine thoroughly & allow to cool before refrigerating tightly covered. Refrigerate several hours before using. (Overcooking may cause the dressing to thicken too much while refrigerated, so it then in that case may be thinned slightly with a little hot water.) Makes 1 1/2-quarts. TO USE THE DRESSING in recreating the salad as served at The Buggy Works, toss together lightly in large bowl:

- 1/2-a-head iceberg lettuce in bite size torn pieces
- about 2 cups endive torn into bite sized pieces
- about 1/2-cup thinly sliced red onion (v-e-r-y thin)
- 1/3 cup (1 small can) Hormel Real Bacon crumbled bits
- 4-oz pkg Kraft's finely shredded Cheddar cheese

Apply only enough of the dressing to lightly but evenly moisten the greens in the above mixture. Let stand 10 mins before serving. Divide between 3 or 4 salad plates. Serve additional dressing on the side. (Makes 3 or 4 servings.)

THIS UNIQUE RESTAURANT turned an old A&P store building into a charming turn-of-the-century atmosphere, complete with high backed booths, brick fireplaces and artifacts of yesteryear, which shows just what a little imagination can do.

BEAN SOUP inspired by The Buggy Works —————————
Over medium heat in medium saucepan combine 1-lb can Campbell brand Pork & Beans, 2 cans (14-oz each) clear chicken broth & 2/3 cup water. Add 1 tsp dry minced onion, 1 TB ketchup, 1 TB finely grated fresh carrot, 1/2-tsp dry minced parsley. Do not allow soup to boil. When heated just till piping hot, serve immediately. makes 3 to 4 servings.

Restaurant successfully duplicated — you can't tell the difference — Perfect

Gloria Pitzer's MAKE ALIKE RECIPES

CREAM OF TOMATO SOUP

It wearies me that canned soups almost always contain MSG, and other unwanted ingredients, so here is a substitute, from scratch, which you can freeze in 10-oz containers to use in place of canned soup in my recipes. Read the labels of the products you use. To my knowledge, only Contadina brand tomato paste contains "only tomatoes".

6-oz can Contadina brand tomato paste
4 cups chicken broth
1 cup instant nonfat dry milk
2/3 cup flour
1-2/3 cups water
salt & pepper

Put 1st 4 ingredients into blender, using half of the broth, blending few seconds or till thoroughly combined. Pour into medium sized-saucepan. Add rest of broth, water. Use wire whisk - med-high just till comes to boil. Get it off the heat before it can scorch, continuing to stir without letting wire whisk touch bottom of pan incase some of soup has indeed scorched a bit. Pour it at once into another pan. Season to taste with salt & pepper & pinch sugar to taste if you wish. Serve promptly. Freeze unserved portions in 10-oz containers, sealing lids in double round of freezer tape, to thaw & use in 6 months in place of 10-oz can tomato soup in my recipes. (1½-qts).

TOMATO SOUP (From Scratch - St. Clair Inn 1950's)

14-oz can stewed tomatoes
6-oz can tomato paste
5-oz (small) can Pet Milk
2 cups water
1 TB onion powder
1 tsp sugar
1/8 tsp baking soda
1/8 tsp garlic salt
1/8 tsp black pepper
4 TB butter or margarine

As listed put into blender, blending high speed just till smooth. Pour into top of double boiler over gently simmering water, cooking & stirring often with wire whisk till piping hot. A minute before serving whisk into hot soup
2 TB sour cream - ½-tsp dry minced parsley
Adjust seasonings to taste with salt, pepper, pinch sugar.

FRENCH BLUE CHEESE DRESSING - Ala St. Clair Inn 1980

Combine 8-oz bottle Kraft's creamy (orange) French Dressing with ¼-cup mayonnaise & ¼-cup crumbled blue cheese. Refrigerate tightly covered to use within a week. Makes 1½-cups.

CREAMY GARLIC DRESSING - Ala St. Clair Inn 1980

Combine 8-oz bottle Wishbone Italian Dressing, 8-oz bottle Wishbone Ranch Dressing. Keep tightly covered & refrigerated to use within a month. makes 2 cups dressing.

made-from-scratch look and taste — *Rules are changing* — *Authentic*

Gloria Pitzer's MAKE ALIKE RECIPES

SIDE DISHES

BAKED BEANS (With Pickle Relish) — Baked Beans

2-lb can Pork & Beans
½-cup Ketchup
½-cup packed brown sugar
½-tsp prepared mustard
4 TB butter or margarine
1 tsp vinegar
1/3 cup Grapenuts or Oat Bran
¼-cup sweet pickle relish

Combine it all in a greased 2-qt baking dish. Crisscross top of dish with strips of partially fried bacon. Bake uncovered at 375F—40 to 45 mins or till bubbly and lightly browned. Serves 4 everso well or 2 shamefully.

DIJON MUSTARD HOMEMADE   Inspired by Grey Poupon

Old-fashioned

2 c dry white wine (Vermouth)
1 cup chopped fresh onion
2 minced cloves unpeeled garlic
4-oz can dry mustard powder
2 TB honey
1 TB oil
2 TB salt
6 drops Tabasco Sauce

Homemade

Combine wine, onion & garlic in small saucepan, bringing to boil for 30 seconds. Reduce heat at once to gentle simmer for 5 mins. Remove from heat. Force mixture through fine mesh strainer. Return the strained mixture to saucepan. With wire whisk, add remaining ingredients, whisking till smooth over medium heat. When mixture looks like a pudding, remove from heat. Cool to lukewarm. Refrigerate in covered container for 24 hours before using. Makes about 2½ cups mustard. Keeps for ages in refrigerator, tightly covered.

SCALLOPED POTATOES
(Inspired by Hudson's 12th Floor Dining Room of the 50's).

The Scalloped Potatoes and baked ham steak was a Thursday-lunch special on the menu of what was once downtown Detroit's finest store!

6 medium potatoes cooked in the jackets (unpeeled),
   cooled, peeled and cubed into bite-sized pieces
10-oz can cream chicken soup
1½-cups shredded Cheddar
¼-cup margarine in bits
1 pint sour cream
1/3 cup chopped green onions

Combine prepared potatoes with remaining ingredients. Spred evenly in greased 9x13x2" baking dish or pan. Then prepare a topping by combining 1 cup fine corn flake crumbs with 4 TB margarine in medium skillet, and sautee till golden, few minutes, med-high heat. Sprinkle evenly over top of potato mixture. Bake uncovered at 350F-about 45 mins or till piping hot and bubbly. Serve immediately. Serves 6 to 8. (Recipe may be cut in half!)

Gloria Pitzer's MAKE ALIKE RECIPES

BAKED POTATO SOUP — BEST-EVER
Slice 4 medium baked, cooled potatoes in half. Scrape out all of pulp into medium saucepan. Freeze shells in plastic bag to use later. Mash pulp with fork. Add 2 cans Campbell's (10-oz each) chicken broth plus 1 broth can water (or use 30-oz homemade chicken broth). Heat on low & add 1 cup half-&-half coffee cream & 2 TB dry minced parsley, 2 TB dry minced onion (or less to taste), ½-tsp hickory flavored salt, ¼-tsp pepper, 2 TB butter, ¼-cup finely minced celery. Heat gently 20 mins. Do NOT boil. Meanwhile fry ½-lb bacon till crispy. Crumble bacon & sprinkle over each of 4 to 6 servings of soup, serving it promptly.

FAST AMERICAN FRIES — SIMPLE
Peel whole boiled-in-their-jackets-potatoes, allowing 1 large potato per serving. Slice into skillet containing enough oil to cover bottom of skillet ¼" deep. Get it hot. What portions of potatœs you can't slice, you can crumble into skillet. Heat till crispy & brown, peeking at underside to check it & then turn to brown otherside. Season to taste with onion salt & pepper.

POTATOES TO MAKE AHEAD
Gently boil round, red skin potatoes, unpeeled till fork tender. (About 45 mins for 6 to 8 potatoes). Refrigerate cooled potatoes in plastic bag to use within a week. Do not freeze.

FRIED POTATO SKINS — OPTIONS — Clever
Using the skins of baked potatoes preferably sliced in half each lengthwise & scraped of all pulp, cut skins into pieces about size of matchbook & drop into 385F- hot oil to fry a minute or two till crispy. Drain & serve promptly with melted cheese and Ranch Dressing for dipping. OR you can use shells cut lengthwise in halves, brushing insides of each in melted margarine & broil on cookie sheet, few inches from broiler heat, just till crispy & brown. Sprinkle at once in shredded Cheddar or drizzle with melted Cheez Whiz & serve promptly.

HASHBROWN SIDEDISH CASSEROLE — VERSATILE
Inspired by Cracker Barrel Restaurant's
Using a greased 9x13x2" baking dish make single layers of the following ingredients: 2-lb bag frozen hashbrowns partially thawed, 1 onion size of a lemon, chopped fine, 6 TB margarine, melted. Then 1-lb sour cream, 8-oz pkg shredded Cheddar cheese & 10-oz can cream chicken soup; sprinkle top in crushed corn flakes. Drizzle in 4 TB melted margarine. Bake 350F 1 hour or till bubbly & piping hot. Refrigerate leftovers. Serves 6 to 8.

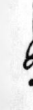

Gloria Pitzer's MAKE A LIKE RECIPES

Chicken Gravy — the gravy
Inspired by Elias Brothers' Big Boy

In blender combine 28-oz chicken broth, ½-tsp onion powder, 1 TB chicken bouillon powder & 2/3 cup Bisquick & blend, high speed, about ½-a-minute or till smooth. Pour into medium saucepan & stir constantly over medium high heat, about 4 or 5 minutes till comes to a boil, is smooth & thickened a bit. Serve at once. Makes 1-quart. (Refrigerate leftovers to warm within a few days or you may freeze gravy to use within 4 months.)

Chicken Pot Pie
Inspired by Fred Sanders – early 1950's

- 2 deep dish unbaked 9" frozen pie shells, thawed
- 2 jars (10-oz ea) chicken gravy
- 1 tsp dry minced onion
- ½-cup frozen peas
- 4-oz can mushrooms
- 6-oz can chunk chicken
- ½-tsp minced parsley
- ¼-cup finely grated fresh carrot

While pie crusts are thawing about 20 mins, prepare filling by combining in large bowl the onion, peas & mushrooms well drained. Break up chicken into bits & add with other ingredients. Wipe bottom of one pie shell with 1 or 2 TB of gravy & bake at 375F-4 mins so crust won't be soggy later. Add filling to partially baked crust, just to rim. Invert the other crust, when thawed over filled pie. Make slits in top. Wipe crust with a bit of melted margarine. Dust in paprika lightly. Bake at 350F- 30 mins or till golden brown & filling bubbles.

SIDE DISH — 3 cheers for fast
CORN SOUFFLE
Inspired by Stouffer's

- 2 eggs
- 2 TB cornstarch
- 2 TB sugar
- Salt & pepper to taste
- Dash of nutmeg
- 1-lb can cream style corn
- ½-cup sour cream
- ½-cup milk

In medium bowl, using electric mixer, high speed, beat eggs till foamy. Beat in each remaining ingredient as listed. Pour into pam-sprayed 8" square baking dish. Bake on center rack of preheated 400F-oven 35 mins or till knife inserted into center comes out clean. Serve promptly. Serves 4 to 6 sensibly.

Gloria Pitzer's MAKE ALIKE RECIPES

RASPBERRY VINAGRETTE - MARTHA'S SALAD
Inspired by Chuck Muer's River Crab Restaurant - St. Clair

- 12-oz jar raspberry jam
- 12-oz water
- ½-cup sugar
- 16-oz white vinegar
- 2 tsp Sweet Basil leaves
- 2 tsp Tarragon leaves
- 4-oz crumbled blue cheese
- ½-cup pine nuts or walnuts
- Shredded Iceberg Lettuce
- Fresh Torn Spinach Leaves
- Thin Slices Red Onion

In small saucepan combine jam, water, sugar. Bring to a boil. Stir till jam melts & sugar dissolves. Remove from heat. Add vinegar, Basil, Tarragon. Cool; refrigerate dressing covered, several hrs before using. To use, strain dressing. Discard leaves & jam seeds. Arrange remaining ingredients on 4 salad plates in appealing fashion. Serve dressing on the side. Serves 4 to 6 well.

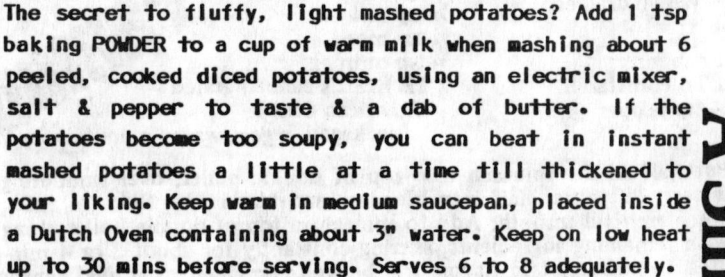

MARY ELIZABETH'S MASHED POTATOES

The secret to fluffy, light mashed potatoes? Add 1 tsp baking POWDER to a cup of warm milk when mashing about 6 peeled, cooked diced potatoes, using an electric mixer, salt & pepper to taste & a dab of butter. If the potatoes become too soupy, you can beat in instant mashed potatoes a little at a time till thickened to your liking. Keep warm in medium saucepan, placed inside a Dutch Oven containing about 3" water. Keep on low heat up to 30 mins before serving. Serves 6 to 8 adequately.

POTATO SALAD FROM BAKED POTATOES

Micro bake 6 large potatoes, making deep "X" through center of each with tip of sharp knife. Arrange 3 at a time, like spokes of wheel, in center of Micro oven. Micro bake on medium, 4-minute intervals, with sheet of paper towel under potatoes. At end of 4 mins, turn each potato over. Micro bake another 4 mins. Turn over again. Repeat till potatoes yield to gentle pressure of fingers, feeling like a fresh orange can feel when you squeeze it. At once place potatoes in pot with tight fitting lid. Let stand 5 mins to continue cooking in their own heat. Slice lengthwise to let cool, cut-side up. Scoop out pulp. Crumble into bits. Combine pulp with 1 cup blender minded celery, ½-cup diced sweet pickle, 1 TB dry minced onion, ½-cup each, mayo, Miracle Whip, sour cream, 1 TB prepared mustard, 1 TB sugar. Refrigerate, covered, to serve in 3 days. Serves 4 to 6.

A Simple Side Dish

Gloria Pitzer's MAKE ALIKE RECIPES

SPINACH QUICHE Inspired by The Ram's Horn Restaurant

9" pie shell unbaked
4-oz can drained mushrooms
10-oz can cream celery soup
2 eggs
¼-tsp nutmeg
½-tsp season salt

1 cup finely shredded
   Swiss cheese
1 TB dry minced onion
10-oz pkg frozen, thawed
   chopped spinach, drained

Partially bake pie shell 6 mins at 375F-. Line pie shell while warm with mushrooms. Put next 4 ingredients into blender high speed few seconds or till smooth. Pour into mixing bowl. Stir in last 3 ingredients. Pour over mushrooms in pie shell. Return to a lowered oven of 350F-to bake almost an hour or till knife inserted into center comes out clean. Serve warm cut in wedges. Serves 6

SPINACH LIKE JOE MUER'S RESTUARANT

15-oz can spinach
   WELL drained
2 eggs
1 cup milk
1 TB cornstarch
½-tsp pepper

1 tsp dry minced onions
½-tsp salt
¼-tsp mace
¾-tsp nutmeg
2 TB Kraft's canned grated
   American Cheese
   (packaged in gold-wrapper container)

Famous

Put half of the spinsach into top of double boiler, over simmering water. Put other half into blender and blend with the eggs, milk, cornstarch till smooth. Add to spinach in top of double boiler along with remaining ingredients, stirring constantly for about 3 or 4 minutes, to make certain flavors will be well combined. Let heat gently till piping hot. Serve in small sidedishes with additional cheese dusted over top of each of 4 servings.

GOOD Pantry — THE VEGETABLE ADVANTAGE
VEGETABLE CASSEROLE

What made this different from other restaurant dishes I have tried is the unique quality of the crispness of the vegetables. The Pantry is not located in Pt. Huron, Michigan anylonger, the way it once was, so I hereby, share this memory with you. To serve 6 sufficiently, slice 1 long thin zucchini, unpeeled, paper thin and mix lightly with 2 cans (1-lb ea) sliced stewed tomatoes, 10-oz box frozen, thawed, broccoli spears, cutting each spear into 4 pieces and 4 ribs celery, sliced paper-thin, half of agreen pepper, seeded and pulp discarded, also sliced paper thin. Then cut a 10-oz pkg frozen cauliflower into small bits about the size of thimbles and add to zucchini mixture. Season lavishly in salt & pepper (or to taste), just a pinch of Rosemary leaves, 1 clove unpeeled garlic, sliced very fine. Cover and bake at 375F— about 45 mins, stirring it once in awhile. Divide mixture then divide mixture equally between 6 Pam sprayed oven-proof soup bowls. Sprinkle ¼-cup shredded Mozzarella over each serving & place bowls 6" from broiler heat in oven just till cheese melts. Serves 6.

Gloria Pitzer's MAKE ALIKE RECIPES

Roast Beef Like Philly's!

A cut above the rest. — Prime Rib

SIRLOIN

Try the technique with a no-rib roast, such as a Sirloin Tip. When you find joy in n-o-t cooking anymore than you have to, this roast practically makes itself and requires only a minimum of attention and details.

7 to 8-lb Sirloin Tip Roast
2 cloves garlic
½-cup oil
½-tsp season salt

Pierce roast with 2-tined carving set fork in 20 or 30 places on all sides. Place cloves of garlic, sliced into halves, in oil, in 12" skillet. Heat oil to almost smoking, remove garlic as soon as it "sizzles"! Heat intensifies the ordor and flavor of garlic, so do not let it remain in the hot oil too long. It might just drive you right out of the kitchen, depending on the strength of the cloves you are using. Aged, dry garlic bulbs have more strength than the freshly picked garlic.

Now brown all sides of roast in hot oil mixture until each side is crispy and place roast, best-side-up on a rack in shallow roasting pan. Bake in preheated 300F—oven, uncovered, 25 minutes per pound, without turning the roast at all during baking—for rare. 30 mins per-lb for med-rare; 35 mins per-lb for med-well and 40-mins per-lb for well. And with that you're on your own—or heading for pot roast possibilities with a well done Sirloin Tip!!! Allow ½-lb per serving. Let roast stand 20 minutes in the roasting pan, before attempting to slice it.

LEFTOVERS may be refrigerated to be used within a week—OR freeze them to be used within 3 months.

STANDING RIB RESTAURANT STYLE

6 to 8-lb standing rib roast
1 clove garlic, slivered

Prepare all surfaces of meat, one side at a time, as follows:

Thoroughly moisten surface of meat with water — pat the water on from faucet with fingers, using pastry brush or draw a wet fork across surface. Sprinkle dry beef marinade or season salt or Mrs. Dash over entire surface of meat, using about ½-tsp per pound. Use salt sparingly as it draws out the natural juice of meat too soon. To insure penetration & retain meat juices, pierce deeply with a kitchen fork at approximately ½-inch intervals. Meat is ready for cooking immediately.

Insert garlic slivers into meat Rub meat with additional spices or herbs of your choice & put roast on rack in shallow pan. Place in preheated 300F—oven & roast total of 18-mins per lb. for rare, 22-mins per lb for medium, 26 mins per lb for med-well. It's best to cut into center thickest part of meat with tip of sharp knife to check juices & color. Take it out of oven a bit sooner than you will like it, as roast continues to cook in its own heat and may be too well-done if you aren't careful! You can always put too rare beef back to roast a bit longer. Let roast stand 10 mins at room temp before you slice it to serve. Each rib will yield 2 generous slices, one with bone & one without!

Gloria Pitzer's MAKE ALIKE RECIPES

Steak Beef

It's Easy. It's Inexpensive.

MARINADE FOR BEEF
Inspired by Steak & Ale

This is a freezer marinade. You put the roast or steaks into the marinade in a freezer container & freeze it to use without thawing within 4 months.

Pierce a 3½-to-4-lb boneless heel of round roast (very little fat & about 2½" thick) with 3-tined fork in about 15 or 20 place. Place the roast in a freezer container with a tight-fitting lid & pour over it: 1 cup V-8 Juice, ¼-cup vinegar, ¼-cup A-1 Sauce, ¼-cup water, ¼-cup Catalina dressing, ½-tsp garlic powder. Seal tightly. Date to use within 4 months. To ½prepare, remove roast from freezer 5 hrs before serving. Loosen roast & marinade in solid chunk from container by running under warm water a minute or two. Place frozen, unthawed chunk in Dutch oven in a 250F-oven, uncovered for 2 hrs. Drain off & discard marinade. Add ¼-cup oil to Dutch oven. Sear roast on high heat top of stove on all sides till crispy-brown. Discard oil. Add then a mixture of **10-oz can cream mushroom soup, 1 cup cranberry juice, 2 TB vinegar, 1 pkg onion soup mix.** Cover with lid. Bake at 250F-3 to 4 hrs depending on size of roast, till meat is so tender it falls apart when touched with a fork. During last hour in the oven, before serving, add: **3 cans (1-lb ea) drained whole potatoes, 3 cxans (15-oz ea) drained whole tiny carrots and 2 cans (1-lb ea) cut green beans, drained plus 2 canws (8-oz ea) mushrooms, drained.** Cover tightly & allow to bake at least an hour before serving. Serves 4 to 6. Leftovers freeze well to thaw & reheat within 4 months. Refrigerate to use in a week, though.

TO MARINATE STEAKS Inspired by Lellie's – of Mich
Use same marinade as given above with 3½-to-4-lbs steaks (any cut) & freeze in tightly sealed container as above for roast. However, to prepare steaks, place frozen chunk of marinade & steaks in pan as you do with roast, in 250F-oven but only till you can loosen meat from marinade. Then discard marinade. Let steaks thaw completely. Pat dry before preparing per your favorite method – broiling or searing.

Steaks

Family Steak

Gloria Pitzer's MAKE ALIKE RECIPES

To keep you up to date

Steaks

TO BROIL - Place on rack in broiler pan, 4" from broiler heat. Allow 6-8 mins per side or till you can cut into center, thickest part of steak & check for color of desired doneness.

TO SEAR STEAKS - Get enough oil in large skillet hot & almost smoking, sufficient only to cover pan evenly (about ¼"). Brown steaks till crispyb on very high heat, both sides, cutting into thickest part of steaks to check for color of desired doneness. Do not over-sear meat as it continues to cook in its own heat when removed from pan to platter.

MEATS

THERE'S NO END TO THE POSSIBILITIES

PERFECT POT ROAST

2½-lbs beef chuck (round bone) "arm" roast
1/3 cup oil
1 envelope onion soup mix
14-oz can clear beef broth
1 onion, the size of an orange, quartered
1-lb fresh carrots peeled & in 3" lengths
5 or 6 medium potatoes peeled & quartered

Preheat oven to 450F-. In a Dutch oven on top of the stove over high heat, quickly sear both sides of the roast in the oil, till crispy-brown. Drain off oil & discard it. Sprinkle soup mix over top of roast. Add broth. Arrange onion pieces & carrots & potatoes over roast. Cover with lid or seal in foil & place in the oven. At once turn oven heat down to 275F-. Allow roast to bake 3½-hours. Turn off oven heat and allow the roast to remain in oven 1 hour. It should remain quite hot. Serves 4 to 6. (Refrigerate covered, cooled roast overnight if you prefer, which allows any fat to come to top & congeal so that it can then be easily removed. You may then add if you wish, 2 cans (10-oz each) mushroom gravy & rewarm. Keep leftovers refrigerated, tightly covered to serve within a week. Freeze in small portions to thaw & use in 4 months.)

Gloria Pitzer's MAKE ALIKE RECIPES

BEEF TIPS ON NOODLES Restaurant Style

Heat together 2 cups bite-sized pieces of leftover pot roast, 3 cans (10-oz ea) mushroom gravy, 10-oz can cream mushroom soup, 8-oz can drained mushrooms, ¼-cup sour cream. Serve piping hot over cooked, drained, still hot, broad egg noodles, allowing 8-oz pkg for 4 nice servings.

SLOW COOKER ALL-NIGHT BEEF ROAST

2 cups water
0.4-oz pkg ranch dressing mix
1 onion size of an orange cut into 4 pieces
3½ to 4-lb heel of boneless round beef roast

As listed put all into slow cooker & cover either with foil till roast shrinks to fit —or with lid. Use HIGH for 4 hours and then LOW for 18 to 20 hours or till roast is fork tender. Let roast stand 15 mins before slicing to serve 6. Freeze leftovers to reheat in 3 months.

AU JUS GRAVY

To serve with sliced beef on toasted rolls, combine in saucepan on medium heat, 14-oz can clear beef broth, 6-oz water (2/3 cup), pinch of onion salt & 10-oz jar Heinz Beef (or Brown) Gravy. Do not let it boil. When piping hot serve in small heat-proof cup in which to dip sandwich. Makes 4 to 6 servings.

Steak Sauce

FILLET MIGNON MARINADE Inspired by Lelli's of Detroit

Mix together equal parts bottled Wine Vinaigrette, V-8 Juice and Catalina dressing. Pierce steaks with tines of fork in many places both sides & submerge in marinade in refrigerator container with tight-fitting lid, 24 hours, turning a few times. Remove from marinade & prepare per your favorite method, searing or broiling.

Fancy Food

ALMOST PERFECT POT ROAST when it's done right

ON PAGE 84 is a Freezer Marinade for pot roast which called for putting the still-frozen chunk of meat & marinade into the oven, etc. I discovered an equally good result from combining the marinade ingredients in a Dutch Oven and then adding the frozen-solid pot roast in 1 piece and followed almost the same procedure from there. Begin by combining in a Dutch Oven: 1 cup V-8 juice, ¼-cup vinegar, ¼-cup A-1 sauce, ¼-cup water, ¼-cup Catalina dressing, ¼-tsp garlic powder. Place frozen 3-lb pot roast in this mixture & place pan on center rack of a preheated 250F-oven 2 hrs. Turn the roast once after 1st hour. Drain off & discard marinade. Add ¼-cup oil to pan around the roast & sear it quickly on high heat on top of stove, all sides, till browned & crispy. Discard oil. Now add 1-lb carrots, peeled & cut into 2" lengths, 4 medium potatoes peeled & quartered, 1-lb can cut-green beans undrained, 8-oz can mushrooms, undrained. Cover with lid. Allow to bake at 250F-4 to 5 hrs depending on size of roast, or till meat is so tender, it falls apart when touched with fork. Serves 4 to 6 favorably. Leftovers freeze well.

POT ROAST ... easiest to make

Meat Loaf — Inspired by BEEF CARVER RESTAURANTS

4 slices white bread
2-lbs ground round
1 cup water
2 eggs
1 pkg onion soup mix
2/3-cup V-8 Juice

Put bread, 1 slice-at-a-time through blender high speed, few seconds till in soft crumbs. Meanwhile put beef into medium mixing bowl & using an electric mixer on med-speed, beat in water, eggs & soup mix. Beat in crumbs. Drop meat into greased Pyrex loaf dish (5½x9x2-3/4"). Bake at 350F- for 30 mins & then add V-8 Juice around the loaf. Return to bake 45 mins longer. Wipe top of meatloaf with a little ketchup, baking 5 mins longer. Let stand 10 mins before slicing to serve 4 favorably or 6 sensibly.

BBQ BEEF SANDWICHES Remembered
(Inspired by Hedge's Wigwam - Royal Oak (Mich) 1950-ish)

I loved this unique restaurant! What I remember best from their cafeteria offerings was the wonderful beef sandwiches, lightly barbecued, on split buns with relish!

You'll need about 4 or 5 cups shredded, cooked beef, from leftover pot roast, preferably, which necessitates cutting leftover lean pieces of pot roast into 2 to 3" cubes while meat is cold and then shredding it into stringlike pieces with tines of a fork. Place in 2½-qt saucepan and add 2 cans (14-oz each) clear beef broth, 1 envelope onion soup mix and 1 cup barbecue sauce. You may use bottled BBQ sauce or my recipe for Hedge's which follows. Let mixture come to a boil and then simmer very gently, uncovered, about 10 mins. Use slotted spoon to apply meat to bun. Top with relish. Serve immediately. makes about 8 generous helpings. Recipe can be doubled & kept warm in slow cooker on low up to 5 or 6 hrs, covered. Leftovers freeze well to thaw & rewarm in 4 months.

BARBECUE SAUCE - All-Purpose
(Inspired by Hedge's Wigwam)

Specialty Restaurant

1 cup ketchup
1 cup Catalina Dressing
1 cup bottled apple butter

1/3-cup Heinz 57 Sauce
2/3 cup V-8 Juice

Combine all ingredients, whisking briskly with wire whisk to mix well. Funnel into bottle with tight fitting cap & refrigerate to use in 30 days. Freeze to thaw & use in 6 months. Makes 1-quart.

Gloria Pitzer's MAKE ALIKE RECIPES

SEASONED French Fries
(Inspired by Hardee's, Rally's and the like!)

Whether it's from Rally's, Hardee's, the local family tavern, these slightly seasoned and lightly batter coated French fries are one of the most often requested recipes on my radio visits and at the TV appearance. Universal Frozen Foods in Boise, Idaho supplies many, many restaurants, both chains & independents with an assortment of ready-to-fry potatoes. They offer either curly or straight, seasoned or plain, some batter-coated, some not. Their "Long Branch Fries" have a remarkable resemblance to those of Rally's and at home I recreate them this way.

Without thawing, open a bag of frozen plain French fries & dust them lightly but evenly in plain flour, letting them dry on waxed paper lined cookie sheet few minutes while you make a thin batter of 1 cup boxed pancake mix & 2 cups Club Soda. We then make a seasoning of ½-tsp black pepper, ½-tsp ground ginger, ¼-tsp dry mustard & 2 TB season salt. Keep that in a tightly covered container, allowing 1 tsp of mixture for each cup of prepared batter. Coat the floured French fries evenly in the batter & fry in small portions at a time in 385F-oil at least 2" deep in an electric fry pan. Turn fries once to brown evenly. Remove with tongs to drain on paper towel lined plate. Serve at once! The batter can be repeated as needed to coat the frozen fries.

FRAJITAS FRIES are merely seasoned as given above with the addition of ½-tsp ground cumin in each cup of prepared batter that includes the seasoning mix given in above recipe.

TWICE BAKED POTATOES

Slice away a 3" oval from tops of 6 med-sized baking potatoes that have been baked till tender. Scoop out pulp into bowl, leaving about ¼" thickness on skins. To the pulp add 1 cup shredded Cheddar, 1 cup sour cream or plain yogurt, 1 tsp dry minced onion (optional) & onion salt to taste, black pepper to taste also. Beat mixture with electric mixer till smooth, adding more sour cream as needed to make creamy consistency. Spoon back into shells, baking any leftover filling in greased custard cups at same time you put potatoes on cookie sheet into 375F- oven about 20-25 mins or till golden brown & puffy. Leftovers do not keep well. Allow 1 potato per serving.

Gloria Pitzer's MAKE ALIKE RECIPES

Onion Rings

ONION BRACELETS
Inspired by Chuck Muer's
Slice white onions ½" thick and separate into rings. Moisten in water & dust in flour. Dip then to coat in wet batter of equal-parts club soda & boxed pancake mix & deep fry at 385F- few min till golden brown & crispy. Remove from oil with tip of knife not tongs! Drain on paper towels. Serve promptly!

Focus On California

ONION BLOSSOM DEEP FRIED — 1990 TRENDS

The new Onion Blossom that is deep fried intrigues me, but at least we can have a Make-Alike at home with this simple technique. Begin by cutting the onion from tip to root end at intervals as you would when you turn a radish into a rose. Slice straight down. Place it in a round frying basket and dust it generously in flour. Shake off excess. Then pour our "Arthur Treacher Fish Batter" Make-Alike batter of equal parts club soda & pancake mix evenly over floured onion "blossom". Let excess drip off onto paper plate. Lower basket into 385F-hot oil in deep fryer few minutes till golden brown & crisp. Lift out of basket with 2 forks. Serve promptly while it's still hot, with chip dip. One onion serves 2 nicely.

An easier version of this appears in our LESS FAT COOKBOOK - 1994

Onion Ring Loaf

ONION RING LOAF (like Tony Roma's)

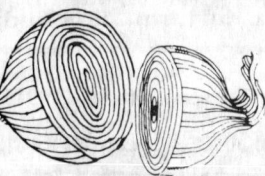

1¼-lbs small white onions (6 or 7)
2 large eggs
2 TB milk
1 to 1-1/3 cups flour
1 tsp salt
1½-pints oil for frying

Slice onions into ¼" rings. Combine eggs & milk in medium bowl. Put flour & salt into large mixing bowl. Heat oil to 385F— in deep fryer or heavy 4-qt saucepan. Dip a deep-frying basket into hot oil & remove to foil lined cookie sheet for awhile. Dip onion rings into egg mixture & then into flour mixture, tossing to coat evenly. Layer rings in basket. Repeat coating rings in egg-mixture & then flour mixture until all have been used & layered into deep frying basket. Press them firmly into basket. Lower basket into hot oil, deep frying 12 to 15 mins or till all rings are browned & crisp. Lift basket from oil. Drain briefly on paper towels. Loosen edges of loaf with knife & invert onto serving plate. Makes 6 servings.

Gloria Pitzer's MAKE ALIKE RECIPES

SHREDDED CHICKEN SANDWICH FILLING
A Unique catering buffet item
Served on a bun like Sloppy Joes

4 or 5 boneless, skinless chicken breasts
3 cans (14-oz ea) clear chicken broth
1 cup minced celery
1 onion the size of an egg, diced fine
1 tsp dry minced parsley
Salt & pepper to taste

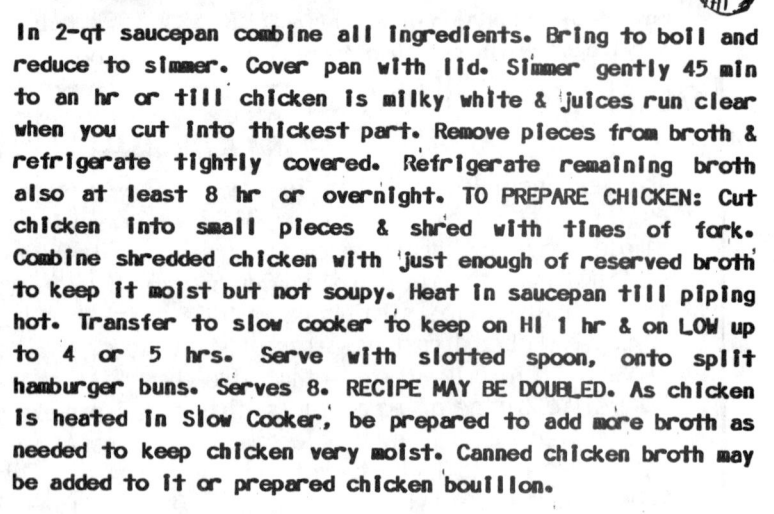

In 2-qt saucepan combine all ingredients. Bring to boil and reduce to simmer. Cover pan with lid. Simmer gently 45 min to an hr or till chicken is milky white & juices run clear when you cut into thickest part. Remove pieces from broth & refrigerate tightly covered. Refrigerate remaining broth also at least 8 hr or overnight. TO PREPARE CHICKEN: Cut chicken into small pieces & shred with tines of fork. Combine shredded chicken with just enough of reserved broth to keep it moist but not soupy. Heat in saucepan till piping hot. Transfer to slow cooker to keep on HI 1 hr & on LOW up to 4 or 5 hrs. Serve with slotted spoon, onto split hamburger buns. Serves 8. RECIPE MAY BE DOUBLED. As chicken is heated in Slow Cooker, be prepared to add more broth as needed to keep chicken very moist. Canned chicken broth may be added to it or prepared chicken bouillon.

SHREDDED CHICKEN Inspired by Chi Chi's
Prepare recipe given above but to the finished mixture in the Slow Cooker, stir in 1 pkg Taco Seasoning mix for 8 servings. Or use a combination of 1 TB chili powder, 2 tsp cumin powder, 2 tsp paprika, ¼-tsp dry mustard, dash of cayenne pepper, dash black pepper or to taste. This mixture seasons 2-qts chicken mixture.

HAM (BOLOGNA) SALAD Inspired by Farmer Jack's (1991)

Into blender put: ¼-cup sweet pickle JUICE, ½-cup MIRACLE WHIP, 6 sweet pickles cut-up, 6 Apple Valley brand Smokey-Links, also cut up & 8-oz sliced bologna in pieces. Using an on/off speed on high, stop motor periodically to clean mixture away from blades, resuming blending until finely minced but not pureed. If necessary remove unfinished mixture into bowl & then blend only ½-cupful at a time. Refrigerate & use in a week. Do not freeze. makes about 2½-cups.

Gloria Pitzer's MAKE ALIKE RECIPES

BBQ Rib Rub **Family Secret**

RIB RUB For Spareribs Barbecued————————————————
Inspired by the East Coast Grill – Cambridge, Mass.

Created by Chris Schlesinger, owner of East Coast Grill, this rib rub technique slow bakes ribs before putting on charcoal grill or under oven broiler heat. I used a dry BBQ Mix made by combining 1 TB season salt, 3 TB packed brown sugar, 1 tsp each: black pepper, chili powder, hickory flavored salt, garlic powder & paprika. Rub on both sides of ribs (3-slabs in 4-bone pieces each). Place meat-side-up in Pam-sprayed oblong baking pans. Bake center rack of 180F- oven 3 hrs without turning. Wrap then in foil & refrigerate up to 2 days. THEN put ribs on rack in highest position over gray coals few mins each side till piping hot or on center rack of oven, turn on broiler heat for few mins & serve heated BBQ sauce on side or spooned over ribs last few mins in oven.————————————
BBQ SAUCE: Mix equal parts bottled apple butter, Catalina Dressing & ketchup.————————————————————————
SUGAR-FREE BBQ SAUCE: Mix 6-oz can tomato paste, 15-oz undrained crushed pineapple in own juice, 10-oz jar of Simply Fruit Cherry Jam & Newman's Own Vinegar-Oil dressing without sugar in it. Heat carefully before served. (Allow ½-lb ribs per serving.)————————————————

original concept

Pre-baked Pizza Crusts

An inspiration
Inspired by Boboli's brand...

The original is $3.39 for a large-size pizza crust. A Make-Alike for half that price is made by thawing a loaf of frozen unbaked bread & dividing it in half, shaping into 2 rounds. Bake on greased pizza pans, one at a time, after rising till doubled, 450F- 15-20 mins or till golden brown. Cool & seal in Ziploc plastic bags. Refrigerate to use in 2 wks or freeze to use in 4 months. TO USE: Bake crust 8 mins at 450F-. Apply heated sauce, Mozzarella & bake 8-10 mins longer or till toppings are bubbly.

Gloria Pitzer's MAKE ALIKE RECIPES

PARTY HAM (Good For Easter!) surprise—

(Bob & Nancy Ballantyne of Toledo, Ohio, serve this wonderfully different baked ham for every special occasion!)

20-lb semi-boneless fully cooked ham
(Herrod or Thorn Apple Valley suggested)

Place ham in shallow roasting pan on lowest rack of oven after having the **broiler** going with oven door closed for 5 minutes. Wipe entire surface of ham in bottled **Open Pit BBQ Sauce (reg'l flavor).** Bob, who masterminds this creation, says that he generously covers the surface of the ham in the BBQ sauce and then leaves it in the oven, door closed, with broiler heat on until you can almost smell the sauce beginning to burn. The sauce will turn dark brown, almost black, and soon as it does, he turns the oven heat **down** to 225F-and leaves it there until the internal temperature of the ham, registers 160 to 165 on a meat thermometer. He doesn't turn the ham and he doesn't baste the ham during this baking time, but when the ham is completely baked, there will be only a very small amount of liquid and fat in the bottom of the pan. The broiler heat will have seared the ham so nicely that all of the juices have been "locked in". Let the ham stand 20 mins on the counter before slicing to serve 20 people. Freeze unused slices in family-sized containers to thaw & rewarm within 4 months. Refrigerate leftovers well covered, to rewarm within a week.

taking ham seriously

Holiday Ham

A FRESH HAM
is prepared like
A PORK ROAST.

Remove it from refrigerator about an hour before baking. Rub surface of ham with clove of garlic. Dust liberally in season salt or Mrs. Dash & dredge in flour. Place fat-side-up on rack in shallow greased baking pan. Place in preheated 450F- oven & at once reduce heat to 325F-, baking uncovered 30-mins-per-lb, depending on degree of doneness desired. If boned, allow 5 mins per pound longer. The internal temperature on a meat thermometer should read 185F-. Let ham stand 15 mins before carving.

Gloria Pitzer's MAKE ALIKE RECIPES

Spicy Buffalo Wings

CAUTION: BUFFALO WINGS MAY BE HABIT FORMING

McFabulous Style or the Colonel's way, the seasoning is the most important factor. To every cup of flour used add ½-tsp ground ginger, ½-tsp black pepper, ¼-tsp dry mustard and 2 TB season salt. Cut off the boney tip of 12 chicken wings & discard & then cut remaining wings at joint. Dip into water & coat in seasoned flour mixture. Fry in very hot oil about 1" deep in heavy skillet till browned both sides. Serve promptly with BBQ dipping sauce or Sweet & Sour Sauce or Blue Cheese dipping sauce. Serves 4 fairly.

For H-O-T style, add dash of Cayenne pepper to flour mixture along with other ingredients. EXTRA CRISPY - use in place of flour, Bisquick. Add seasonings to that as above.

HAM CROQUETTES — Inspired by Bill Knapp's

Put 2 to 2½-cups leftover shredded baked ham (or canned Chunk Ham), shredded finely into a 10" skillet with just enough water to cover ham. Put a lid on the skillet & simmer about 10 mins. Drain. Reserve liquid, adding only enough more water to this to give you to cups total. Combine that 2 cups of liquid with the ham in large mixing bowl. Add 1 envelope onion soup mix, 2 beaten eggs, 1 tsp onion powder, ½-tsp poultry seasoning, ½-tsp dry minced parsley. Work in about 2½-cups dry fine bread crumbs or enough crumbs that you can form mixture into 3" high cones, shaping these between the palms of your hands. Dredge each completely but lightly in plain flour. Dip to cover them next in slightly beaten egg & dash of water mixed together. (Flavored croutons can be put through blender to fine crumbs to use for more flavor - any flavor of your choice.) Use equal parts oil & margarine, about ½" deep in skillet on medium high heat in which to brown the croquettes, on all sides & then transfer carefully, widest ends down, side-by-side in Pam-sprayed 9" square baking dish or baking pan. Bake uncovered 350F- (for both glass or metal baking pan), about 15 to 20 mins or till piping hot & nicely browned. Spoon a little white sauce over each croquette just before serving, allowing 2 croquettes per person. Serves 6.

NOTE: Freeze leftover croquettes to thaw & reheat gently in Microwave or in pan covered in foil, in conventional oven, 400F- 12-15 minutes or till piping hot.

WHITE SAUCE FOR CROQUETTES: Into blender put 1½-cups cold water, ½-cup non-fat milk powder, 1/3 cup flour. Blend high speed few seconds till smooth. Pour into small saucepan & cook on med-high, stirring constantly till smooth & thickened. Remove at once from heat & stir in 2 TB butter or margarine & salt & pepper to taste.

Buffalo Wings — the main dish

Gloria Pitzer's MAKE ALIKE RECIPES

STUFFING SKILLET STYLE like Sveden House

- 1/4-cup oil
- 2 ribs celery sliced thin
- 8-oz can mushrooms undrained
- 1 cup raisins
- 1 tsp dry minced onion
- 1 tsp dry minced parsley
- 1 TB rubbed sage
- 2 TB beef bouillon powder
- 2 cups water
- 10 slices bread crumbled

In medium skillet heat oil & add each ingredient as listed, on med-heat, stirring till bread absorbs all liquids. Then on low heat, cover pan & let cook till celery is tender & flavors have mellowed. OR transfer to greased 2-qt baking dish. Cover in foil & bake 350F- 25-30 mins. Serves 6.
OYSTER STUFFING OPTION - In place of mushrooms use 1/2-pt oysters, chopped plus liquid in which it is purchased.

idea catches on

Bob Ovens CHICKEN 'N NOODLES

No one else has this specialty but Bob Evans

Not a gravy, but a light broth, laced with homemade noodles—or use a pkg of Polish style wide egg-noodles.

- 3 cans (14-oz each) clear chicken broth
- 1 broth can of water
- 2 ribs celery diced fine
- 2 TB dry minced onion
- 1 medium raw carrot grated on large hole of vegetable grater
- 3 cups dry wide egg noodles
- 6½-oz can boned chicken, undrained

Combine broth & water in 2½-qt saucepan and bring just to a boil. Add remaining ingredients, reducing heat to gentle simmer, uncovered, for 20 mins or till noodles are tender. Serve as you would a soup. Serves 4. Leftovers can be refrigerated to rewarm in a week. Freeze to thaw & reheat in 3 months.

time-honored family recipe
MOM'S HOME COOKING

Mom used to make — dishes that you don't always find in restaurants, but sometimes wish you did.

TUNA NOODLE CASSEROLE

- 2 qts water
- ½-tsp salt
- 4 cups dry, uncooked broad egg noodles
- 10-oz can cream of celery soup
- 10-oz can cream of chicken soup
- ½-cup (Kraft's) bottled buttermilk dressing
- 6½-oz can tuna
- 1 TB dry minced onion
- 2 TB sweet pickle relish
- 1 cup finely crushed O'Grady's Au Gratin potato chips (about 1/3 of a 10-oz bag)

Bring water to boil with salt in 4-qt kettle. Drop in noodles and cook at a gentle boil, about 12 to 15 mins or till tender. Drain but do NOT rinse. While the noodles are cooking, combine remaining ingredients, EXCEPT potato chip crumbs, in 2-qt mixing bowl. Add hot, drained noodles, coating lightly in soup mixture. Turn into Pam sprayed 9" square baking dish. Spread crushed potato chips evenly over top. Bake at 350F—about 30 mins or till bubbly. Serves 4 to 6 lovingly!
(Refrigerate leftovers, well-covered, to rewarm within 3 or 4 days. Do not freeze!)

Gloria Pitzer's MAKE ALIKE RECIPES

≈950

MARINADE FOR STEAKS & CHICKEN
Inspired by Kensington Club's & likewise Steak & Ale's

FOR STEAKS
- ½-cup ketchup
- ½-cup tomato juice
- ¼-cup red wine
  or purple grape juice

FOR CHICKEN OR PORK
- ½-cup soy sauce
- ½-cup pineapple juice
- ¼-cup white wine
  or white grape juice

With either combination of ingredients, combine the 4 ingredients listed & marinate meat in mixture, refrigerated & tightly covered 24 hrs. Remove from marinade & prepare, per your favorite recipe. Either recipe makes 12-oz.

(STEAK & ALE it appears may add dash Worcestershire to the ingredients for marinating steaks.)

MACARONI & CHEESE
Inspired by Beef Carver Restaurants

Consistently Good

Into blender put 14-oz can clear chicken broth & 1/3 cup of cornstarch. Blend high speed till smooth. Pour into medium saucepan. Cook, stirring constantly with wire whisk on high heat till comes to boil & is thickened & smooth. Remove at once from heat. Stir in 16-oz jar Cheez Whiz & ¼-tsp dry-mustard, 2/3 cup sour cream. Combine with 1-lb box elbow-macaroni, cooked till tender, per box directions, drained well, but not rinsed. Refrigerate leftovers to serve within a week. Freeze to thaw & use within 4 months. Serves 6.

NOODLES ALFREDO Inspired by Betty Crocker's

About ½-hour before serving cook an 8-oz pkg fettucini or medium egg noodles per pkg directions till tender. Meanwhile in a large mixing bowl that you have first rinsed out in hot water to warm it up, combine 4 TB grated Parmesan, 4 TB butter or margarine, 2 TB light coffee cream or buttermilk or even use 1 TB sour cream with 1 TB milk. Stir till smooth. Add a dash salt and pepper to taste. Soon as noodles are cooked, drain & toss them to coat in the creamy mixture. Additional Parmesan can be sprinkled over each serving. Serves 4.

ALFREDO SAUCE FOR THE NOODLES

One more way to create the sauce is while the fettucini is cooking, in a medium skillet, melt 4 TB of margarine and 3-oz pkg cream cheese with 1/3 cup milk stirring till completely smooth over low heat. Don't let it boil or it may curdle. Remove from heat and beat in with wire whisk, 4 TB grated Parmesan. Then soon as noodles are cooked & drained, combine the fettucini with the warm sauce, coating it well and sprinkling top of each serving in more Parmesan.

Pasta as a Side Dish

Gloria Pitzer's MAKE ALIKE RECIPES

Bacon

BACON PROPERLY PREPARED - less greasy...

Comparing notes with a number of conscientious cooks, it looks like the desired result is not so much the outcome of a recipe faithfully followed but the cut of the bacon, amount of leanness, degree of heat & attention of the cook.

Some insist bacon curls in the pan if the heat is too high. Even the technique of properly separating the strips from a package of supermarket bacon remains a questionable practice. Accordingly, one begins by rolling the bacon up jelly-roll-style across top of "the slab" of strips as far as you can roll. Then unroll it and reverse it by turning slab over & rolling it up in the other direction beginning at other end of slab. The slices should then (but they don't always) separate, neatly & easily. Placed side-by-side in roomy skillet over med-high heat, it is FRIED (oh, that dubious word that makes nutritionists cringe...)till almost transparent, then turned & fried till the transparent areas begin to brown. To remove excess fat while bacon is frying, one can soak it up with very absorbant wads of paper toweling or pieces of day old bread. The less fat in the skillet, the less spattering occurs. Each slice, as it browns to crispness, should then be removed with tongs or a 2-tined fork, to drain on paper towels. At some diners the bacon strips are also pressed between cotton towels. It's always perfect, but then it's a matter of taste, isn't it?...Crispy...wiggly...chewy...dry...

LASAGNA like Roma Hall (Detroit) 1960's & 70's
A banquet & catering enterprise

Butter a 10" or 12" (3" deep) baking dish or souffle dish. Cut 10 large cooked lasagna noodles each in half. Set aside. Ladle 1 cup hot, rich spaghetti sauce into bottom of baking dish to cover bottom evenly. Arrange about a third of noodles over sauce in single layer. Spread thinly sliced Mozzarella cheese over this. Add more sauce just enough to cover cheese, then 1/2 of the remaining noodles. Sprinkle about ½-cup grated Parmesan over this. Put 1 cup cottage cheese through blender with 1 egg, using high speed a few seconds, just till smooth. Spread this on top of Parmesan layer. Add the last of the noodles, more sauce to cover, another layer of Mozzarella, an even sprinkling of additonal Parmesan and a 4-oz can well-drained mushrooms right in the center of the top of the dish. Then arrange strips of additional Mozzarella cheese like the spokes of a wheel around the mound of canned mushrooms. Bake uncovered at 350F about 25 to 30 mins or till cheese is melted and Lasagna is hot and bubbling. Serves 6 to 8 adequately or 3 foolishly!

Spaghetti Sauce
Inspired by Chuck Muer Restaurants

SHORT-CUT

Spaghetti

- 1-to-1½-lbs ground round
- 1/8 cup oil
- 1 long rib celery diced
- 1 lg tomato peeled & diced
- 1 onion size of egg diced
- 1 cup V-8 juice
- ½-medium green pepper diced (optional)
- 14-oz can stewed tomatoes, cut-up
- 2 TB beef bouillon powder
- ½-cup grape jelly
- 27-oz can Hunt's spaghetti sauce
- ¼-tsp baking soda

In 2-qt saucepan brown beef in oil, high heat and add celery, tomato & onion. Saute 5 mins. Add each remaining ingredient EXCEPT soda. Stir frequently. Bring just to boil Turn at once to low. Stir in baking soda which cuts acidity & smooths out the sauce nicely. Allow to cook gently on low 30 min. Makes (2-qts). Freezes well to use in 6 months.

Pierogies

Make a soft dough of 4 cups flour, ½-tsp cream of tartar and 2 TB oil, with about 1 cup of lukewarm skimmed milk, sufficient to knead it with lightly floured hands into smooth texture. Cover the dough and let it rest 30 minutes. Prepare the filling in the meantime, which she suggested —

Saute 1/3 cup finely chopped fresh onion in 1 TB oil till transparent. Do not brown the onion. In small bowl beat together ¾-cup leftover, cold mashed potatoes with ¾-cup cottage cheese and salt and pepper to taste. Add the sauteed onion. Roll the dough out quite thin, in small portions at a time. Don't let dough be so thin that it will split, though. Cut with floured biscuit cutter or round cookie cutter into 2½-to-3" circles. Working with floured hands, place a circle of the dough in the palm of the hand and put about a teaspoon of the filling in the center. Fold the circle in half and pinch or press edges together to seal it well. Place these in single layer on damp towel. Cover until all pieces have been prepared. Drop a few at a time into slightly salted and gently boiling water to boil about 5 minutes or till tender. Remove from water with slotted spoon. Drain a few minutes and serve promptly with a topping of 1 part melted butter and 3 parts sour cream. Makes about 3½-dozen.

FOR A MEAT FILLING FOR PIEROGI·

To the mashed potato mixture in above recipe you can also add 1-lb well browned, crumbled ground beef mixed well with 1 beaten egg, increasing onion to taste. You can also brown "hot" and well-spiced bulk-style breakfast sausage, allowing about a pound for above recipe. Drain the browned and well crumbled sausage and combine with potato mixture, adjusting seasonings to taste.

Sandwich

CHEESE FRENCHIE BATTER COATED SANDWICH

Some 30 years ago this unique sandwich was really popular. Place 2 slices American Cheese (like Kraft's Singles) between 2 slices white bread. Cut in half diagonally. Brush lightly the outside surface of bread in a little milk & dust lightly in plain flour. then make a batter out of equal parts Club Soda & boxed pancake mix & using 2 forks, dip one half of the sandwich at a time into a shallow dish containing the prepared batter, coating sandwich evenly. At once place in electric skillet containing at least an inch of hot oil at 385F- & fry till browned turning once to brown both sides.———

Cheese Sauce for Vegetables Great Sauce

Into blender put 14-oz can clear chicken broth & ¼-cup cornstarch. Blend high speed few seconds. Pour into saucepan & cook on high heat, stirring constantly with wire whisk till comes to boil. Continue stirring while it boils ½-minute. Remove from heat. Add 16-oz jar Cheez Whiz micro-melted per jar label directions. Add ½-tsp dry mustard. Refrigerate tightly covered to use in 2 weeks or freeze to thaw & rewarm within 6 months.———

MACARONI & CHEESE

Prepare the Cheese Sauce For Vegetables (above) adding also to the sauce 2/3 cup sour cream, ½-tsp dry minced parsley, ½-cup finely minced celery & 1-lb box elbow macaroni, cooked till tender & drained but not rinsed. Rewarm in microwave or over hot water or in 350F-oven till piping hot, but NOT over direct heat. Serves 6.———

Affordable

Marinated Chicken Breast
Chicken Fillets
Inspired by Ya Ya's

Marinate boneless skinless chicken pieces in a combination of ¼-cup Heinz 57 Sauce, ¼-cup lime juice, ¼-cup orange juice & 1 cup water. Repeat recipe sufficiently to cover chicken pieces in a non-metallic container with tight fitting lid. Refrigerate 24 hrs, removing then chicken. Discard marinade. Place pieces on broiler pan about 4 to 6 inches from heat. Brush with melted margarine & broil both sides till done, about 4 to 5 mins each side.

WHITE PIZZA

GOOD

- 8-oz tube Crescent Dinner Rolls
- 1/4-cup bottled Ranch Dressing
- 1/2-cup sour cream
- 3-oz pkg cream cheese, softened
- 1 tsp dry minced onion
- 1/2-lb crispy fried, crumbled bacon
- 1 cup cooked, drained chopped broccoli
- 8-oz can mushrooms drained
- a little fresh, finely grated carrot
- a little minced parsley flakes

Open dinner roll dough & unwrap into 1 sheet, fitting it carefully into Pam sprayed jelly roll pan, stretching it a bit with fingers to fit side-to-side. Pinch seams and seal. Bake at 375F- about 10 mins or till well browned & fully baked. Cool in pan on rack 5 mins. Mix together the dressing, sour cream, cream cheese & onion & spread over crust. Arrange other ingredients evenly over creamy layer. Serve it cold, cut into squares. You can also sprinkle a little shredded Mozzarella over top of it all & put it a few inches from broiler heat just to melt cheese if you wish, but we liked it without it. Serves several!

Italian Cooking

EGGPLANT PARMIGIANA
Inspired by The Olive Gardens

Olive Garden

Peel & slice an eggplant into $\frac{1}{4}$" thick slices. Moisten slices & coat lightly in flour. Quickly brown slices in hot oil in heavy skillet, dusting each side generously in season salt. When fork tender & golden brown transfer to jelly roll pan. Cover loosely in foil & bake at 375F-about 20-25 mins or till tender. Meanwhile prepare sauce. Allowing 2 slices eggplant per serving, prepare 8 slices for this amount of sauce. In medium saucepan combine 1-lb jar PREGO meat-flavored spaghetti sauce, 1/3 cup grape jelly, 14-oz can sliced style stewed tomatoes, broken up with fork. Heat on medium till piping hot. Do not boil. Be sure jelly is melted. Arrange 2 slices prepared eggplant on each of 4 dinner plates. Cover each slice eggplant with thin slice Mozzarella. Then ladle spaghetti sauce over all, not to cover completely, though. Place plates in 375F-oven just to melt cheese & serve promptly. Serves 4.

Gloria Pitzer's MAKE ALIKE RECIPES

SPAGHETTI SAUCE — (With Grape Jelly)

In heavy 2½-qt saucepan, on medium-high heat, brown 1½-to-2-lbs ground round in 4 TB oil, crumbling with fork till pink color disappears. Turn heat to low & stir in 14-oz can sliced style stewed tomatoes, 1-lb jar Prego Spaghetti Sauce, 1½-oz envelope onion soup mix, 6-oz can V-8 Juice & ½-cup grape jelly. Cook uncovered on low 30 mins. Serve over 1-lb cooked, drained thin spaghetti. Serves 4.

More Than You Expect!

White Clam Pasta Sauce

HUDSON'S CLAM PASTA SAUCE

Drain the liquid from a 10-oz can minced clams into 2-qt saucepan. Cut all of the larger pieces of clams into small pieces & add to the liquid. Then add 1-qt rich chicken broth, ½-cup fresh chopped parsley, 1 clove garlic-finely minced & ½-tsp onion powder. Heat it thoroughly and serve the sauce on the side with cooked, drained, hot pasta (either very thin spaghetti or Mostaccioli) and sprinkle the top of the sauce with a generous spoonful of grated Parmesan. Sufficient to cover a 1-lb box pasta—cooked & drained.

SPAGHETTI SAUCE (Fresh Tomatoes)
Inspired by Ragu

Drop about 15 large ripe tomatoes into boiling water briefly & then into ice water briefly to loosen skins so you can peel them clean. Cut them up fine in 2½-qt saucepan & simmer slowly with 1 TB salt, stirring constantly till draws a liquid (about 1 hour). Force mixture through strainer to remove seeds. Return to pan or slow-cooker to cook on low heat, cautiously so doesn't scorch. When reduced in volume to sauce, measure the sauce & for each quart stir in 2 TB brown sugar, ½-tsp garlic powder, ¼-cup minced onion, 2 TB beef bouillon powder, 1 TB dry oregano leaves, 3 TB of ketchup, ¼-tsp black pepper, ¼-cup of grape jelly, ¼-cup sweet pickle relish & ¼-cup minced green pepper. When the flavor is suitable, remove from heat. Divide between freezer containers with tight-fitting lids, leaving 1" headspace & seal in masking tape. Freeze & use in 6 months.

AMAZING — UNIQUE — Fresh Frozen Spaghetti

Gloria Pitzer's MAKE ALIKE RECIPES

PASTA PRIMIVERA
(River Crab Restaurant - St. Clair, Mich.)

Put 2-oz garlic (by weight) into blender with 40-oz olive oil (by measure) & emulsify (or use Food Processor), high speed just till smooth. Add 6-oz (by weight) "Clam Base"(*) and 24-oz (my measure) hot water. Blend till well combined. Transfer to Dutch Oven or kettle. Keep on lowest possible heat just to warm—not "cook". Stir in 3-oz (by measure) fresh chopped parsley. Combine this sauce with 4-oz fresh chopped vegetables (**- as given below) that have been sauteed in 3-oz oil just to "crisp".
(*) Clam base can be made at home from equal parts bottled clam juice and canned clam broth. If clam broth is not available put 6-oz can undrained clams through blender high speed just till smooth (few seconds). Add ½-cup boiling water to pureed clam mixture. Measure out to use in place of required "clam base".
(**) Fresh vegetables include:
   Bok Choy
   Pea Pods
   Red Onions
   Red (sweet) peppers

Mangia!

(** more vegetables)
Diced fresh tomatoes (occasionally,
Carrots sliced in matchstick pieces
Green (Bell) peppers
Fresh sliced mushrooms
Celery sliced thin

To the above vegetable mixture add equal measure of cooked, drained pasta (any style or shape but thicker pieces are preferred.)
This will serve 30 to 34.

HOMEMADE NOODLES & PASTA DOUGH

2¼-cups all-purpose flour
2 eggs
4 TB cold water
1 TB corn oil
1 tsp salt

Pasta Perfect Perfectly Fresh

Put flour into large mixing bowl. Beat eggs together with remaining ingredients. Make well in center of flour and pour in liquid mixture. Work mixture together to form smooth, stiff dough. Knead till smooth with lightly floured hands in bowl —or on floured surface. Must be smooth and not one bit sticky, but don't over-do on flour or the dough will crumble. Wrap dough in plastic food bag and leave it alone at room temperature, for about 30 minutes.

TO USE NOODLE DOUGH:
   Cut the portion of above prepared dough into 2 equal parts. Roll one half of dough at a time on floured surface to 1/16" thickness—really THIN. Fold dough over in half and then in half again. Slice through these 4 folds with sharp knife to make ¼" wide slices, unwrapping into noddles. Dry the noodles at least an hour before dropping into slightly salted boiling water to cook till tender (about 12 to 14 minutes, depending on thickness)— or dry till brittle and store in covered containers at room temperature to use within 6 months.

Makes about 1-pound of noodles.

(For very thin soup noodles, keep slices as narrow as possible since cooking in simmering, slightly salted water, will cause noodles to triple in bulk.)

Gloria Pitzer's MAKE ALIKE RECIPES

EXCEPTIONAL

STEAK AND SHAKE CHILI — St. Louis Style!

On our way home from Branson, Missouri, we stopped in St. Louis for gas and across the highway I spotted a Steak And Shake unit. I braved the traffic and ran over there, returning with a carry out of their famous chili. It has been many years since I sampled this unique dish. To recreate it at home I would brown about 1½ to 2-lbs ground round in a few TB oil in 2½-qt heavy saucepan, crumbling beef with fork till the pink color disappears. Then I would stir in 14-oz can clear beef broth, 2 broth cans of water and a 6-oz can tomato paste, stirring till smooth. I would add 1 TB Hershey's syrup, ½-tsp instant coffee powder (decaf or reg'l), 1 TB chili powder & 2 tsp cumin powder, ¼-tsp garlic powder, ¼ tsp oregano powder, ½-tsp season salt, 3-cans (1-lb each) red kidney beans, undrained. Heat gently till piping hot, but do not let it boil. Serve sincerely to six!

CONEY ISLAND CHILI (No Beans)
Inspired by Lafayette Chili & Greek Coney Island Sauce

In deep skillet brown 1- 1½-lbs ground round in ½-cup oil till pink color disappears. Mash with fork to consistency of rice. Meanwhile into blender put ½-cup water, 14-oz can clear chicken broth, 1 tsp ground cumin, 1 tsp turmeric, 1 TB chicken bouillon powder, 6-oz V-8 juice. Blend high speed few seconds till smooth. Pour into skillet, stirring constantly med-high, till smooth & thickened. Remove 2 cups mixture to blender. Blend high speed till smooth. Return to remaining mixture in skillet. Serve promptly. Serves 4 generously!

HORN MILL CHILI Inspired by Hormel's
A good basic chili with no beans!

1-lb ground round steak	2 tsp chili powder
1 TB oil	1 tsp cumin powder
1 envelope onion soup mix	1/2-tsp Worcestershire
1-lb jar spaghetti sauce	1/4-cup cooking wine
1-lb can stewed tomatoes	or white grape juice

In 2½-qt skillet, brown beef in oil, crumbling it with fork till size of rice, medium high heat, till pink color disappears from beef. Stir in then each remaining ingredient as listed. Cook on lowest possible heat uncovered, stirring once in awhile for 2 hrs. Serves 4. (1-lb can UNDRAINED red beans can be added 20 mins before cooking time is up if you like.)

Gloria Pitzer's MAKE ALIKE RECIPES

CHIMICHANGA GRAVY/SAUCE Inspired by Chi Chi's

Mix together 10-oz jar Heinz brown gravy & 10-oz Heinz turkey- or-chicken gravy, plus 1 TB finely chopped canned green chills & heat gently till piping hot. Spoon over fried, filled burritos. Garnish in shredded green pepper. Makes 2½-cups

UNEQUALED

SPANISH RICE
Inspired by Chi Chi's

In medium skillet heat together: 1 c bottled Chi Chi's mild salsa with 1 cup V-8 Juice just till comes to the boil. Remove from heat. At once stir in 1 c Minute Premium Rice. Cover pan with tight-fitting lid. Let stand 6 to 8 mins or till rice is tender. Fluff with fork. Serve promptly. Makes 4 ample servings.

CATFISH OVEN-STYLE

This is the official main-dish of Branson, Missouri!

3½-to-4-lb skinned and boned catfish
½-tsp season salt
2 cups seasoned croutons
1 TB dry minced parsley
1 TB sweet pickle relish
2 TB dry minced onion
1 egg beaten
Salt & Pepper as you wish
2 TB margarine, melted
6 slices lean salt pork
Basting Broth (see below)

Rinse fish in cold water & pat dry with paper towels. Wipe cavity in season salt. Combine croutons, parsley & relish, onion, egg & salt & pepper & spoon into the cavity of fish. Secure with skewers to close fish, or lace in string. Wipe surface in margarine. Make 3 slits on each side & insert a strip of salt pork into each slit. Place fish in greased baking dish. Bake uncovered, 350F—about an hour basting every 10 mins in basting broth. (See below)

BASTING BROTH

A perfect seasoning broth to use when baking fish or chicken.

In small saucepan on medium heat, combine 1½-cups water, 4 thin slices fresh lemon, 1 slice of an onion about size of orange & 1 bay leaf crumbled, plus ½-cup diced celery including leaves & 4 peppercorns or ½-tsp black pepper. Bring to boil. Reduce to gentle simmer. Cover pan. Simmer gently 20 mins. Strain & reserve clear broth for basting. Makes about 1-2/3 cups.

GREEN CHILI Mexicali
Like Chili's

Almost every Mexican Taco Shop has their own version of this specialty, usually served on a Burito shell.

1-lb ground round
2 TB oil
½-tsp season salt
¼-tsp black pepper
14-oz can clear chicken broth
3 ribs celery (each about 12" long and in 1" pieces)
1 med-lg green pepper seeded and cut into 4 or 5 pieces
Leaves only of 1 bunch fresh parsley
Bulbs & stems of 4 green onions
1 TB dry minced cilantro
1 tsp ground coriander
1 tsp garlic powder
¼-tsp Tabasco Sauce
1/3 cup fine corn chip crumbs

Brown the beef in the oil in large skillet. Add everything else. Cook uncovered, stirring often, for 30 mins. Serves 6. Leftovers freeze well.

Gloria Pitzer's MAKE ALIKE RECIPES

CHINESE EGG ROLLS

The Batter:
2 cups flour
1 egg
½-tsp salt

The Filling:
¼-cup corn oil
½-cup finely chopped celery
¼-cup finely chopped green onions
¼-tsp garlic powder
1 cup chopped cooked shrimp
1 cup chopped leftover pork roast
1 cup finely chopped water chestnuts
1 cup bean sprouts
¼-cup soy sauce
½-tsp powdered ginger
1 tsp sugar

Prepare the batter by gradually adding 2½ cups water to the flour, beating into a smooth batter, adding the egg and salt. Refrigerate 1 hour before using.

To Prepare The Filling:
Put the oil in heavy skillet and saute the celery & onions till tender. Add remaining ingredients as listed. Stir and fry on low heat till thoroughly heated. Set it aside.

The egg roll skins are prepared a bit like a tortilla or a thin tiny pancake. Grease a non-stick surfaced skillet & get it quite hot, using only 2 TB batter for each egg roll skin. Turn the pan like you would a crepe to get the batter to spread evenly and thinly over the skillet, doing only 1 or 2 at a time. Cook them but do not let them brown. Stack them with a sheet of waxed paper between each one till all have been cooked. Keep skillet greased well inbetween each egg roll.

Place a TB or so of filling in center of each pancake. Fold 4 sides over it and turn seam sides down on cookie sheet to let them cool while you heat a pint of corn oil to 400 degrees. You really must use a wire frying basket to work well. Place only enough of the filled egg rolls over the bottom of the frying basket that they will not touch each other and make a single layer (about 3 or 4 at a time). Lower the basket carefully into the hot oil and allow to brown a few minutes. Lift the basket out. Let excess oil drip back into pan. Lift each egg roll out carefully with tongs to drain on paper.

PIZZA ROLLS

Prepare the batter per directions for Egg Rolls.

The filling consists of:
Brown 1-lb Italian breakfast style sausage in bulk form, crumbling it with a fork as it browns, without any additional fat in a hot skillet. When tender, add:
1 tsp dry oregano leaves
¼-tsp garlic powder
¼-cup chopped onions
½-tsp chili powder

Stir to blend & remove from heat. Add 8-oz can drained & then chopped mushrooms, ½-cup pizza sauce, or bottled Prego Spaghetti Sauce with meat flavoring or mushroom flavoring. Stir in 2 TB grated Parmesan and spoon it by a tablespoonful into center of each cooked but not yet browned egg roll skin. Fold over the 4 sides as in Egg Roll Recipe, deep frying these in French frying basket in hot oil till crispy and browned. Drain on paper toweling a few minutes. Place in single layer on baking sheet & place uncovered in freezer for a few hours or till firm. Then quickly wrap them in plastic freezer containers to be used within 3 months. TO SERVE THE PIZZA ROLLS—thaw and brown in a 425F—oven for 8 to 10 minutes or till crispy. Add a hot sauce on the side.

PIZZA ROLL SAUCE:

Mix together 10-oz bottle chili sauce, ¼-cup horseradish, 2 TB sugar, 2 TB lemon juice, ½-cup ketchup. Stir to blend well. Makes about 1¾-cups sauce.

Gloria Pitzer's MAKE ALIKE RECIPES

Mc FABULOUS CHICKEN FAJITAS

6 flour tortillas lightly browned on oiled griddle and kept soft in colander over simmering water (10 min)

2 boneless, skinless chicken breasts
½-cup finely slivered green pepper
¼-cup finely diced onion
1 medium tomato diced fine
1 TB Mexican Seasoning (recipe follows)
4-oz pkg finely shredded Cheddar cheese

To keep you up to date

While tortillas are steaming, place whole chicken breasts in medium skillet with green pepper, onions, diced tomatoes & seasoning. Simmer covered 10 mins. With slotted spoon remove chicken breasts to lightly oiled griddle or shallow skillet & brown briskly both sides, few mins, high heat. With slotted spoon remove green peppers, onion & tomatoes from liquid & add to chicken. Keep mixture on low heat, cutting chicken into bite-sized pieces. Divide mixture equally between the 6 soft tortillas. Divide Cheddar cheese equally over that. Fold sides of tortilla toward center & seal in filling, shaping folded tortilla into a roll. Serve with mild salsa & sour cream on the side.

our secret

MEXICAN SEASONING

1 TB chili powder
1½-tsp ground cumin
½-tsp ground coriander
½-tsp cilantro leaves
   rubbed to fine dust between fingers
1 tsp instant tea powder
½-tsp dry minced parsley
½-tsp black pepper
¼-tsp garlic salt
¼-tsp onion salt

Combine all ingredients & sift together 3 times. Funnel into bottle with tight fitting cap. Keep out of direct sunlight to use in 6 months. Refrigerate to use in 1 year. Makes about 3 TB of seasoning.

TACO SEASONING FOR BEEF:

Combine 1 recipe of Mexican Seasoning (recipe above) with 1 tsp dry mustard, 1 tsp ground turmeric, 1 tsp sugar, 1 TB of paprika, 1 TB season salt. Use 2 TB of this mixture to season 1-lb to 1½-lbs ground beef, as you brown it in a little oil just till pink color disappears, crumbling beef with fork till completely browned, but overdone.

tastes virtually the same

Gloria Pitzer's MAKE ALIKE RECIPES

FISH BROILING Restaurant-Style

Spray a jelly roll pan lightly in Pam. Place a nice piece of fish skin-side-down – meaty side up – on pan. Wipe top of fish evenly in squeeze bottle margarine or melted butter. Dust lightly in paprika. Then rub dry parsley leaves between your fingers to a fine dust, evenly over top of fish. Drizzle in a little lemon juice. Place 4 to 6 inches from boiler heat. Do NOT turn fish. Broil only 4 to 6 mins, depending on thickness of fish, or until you can flake fish easily with a fork and it appears milky white in color. Do NOT overcook fish or it will be tough. Serve immediately with lemon wedges & tartar sauce. Allow $2\frac{1}{2}$-3-lbs fish for 4 servings. If frozen, thaw completely & prepare promptly. Keep fish refrigerated until time to prepare & serve.

Almond Chicken — Perfect OF THE ORIENT

3 cups Club Soda
3 cups boxed pancake mix
1 tsp dry mustard
½-tsp season salt

1½-cups all-purpose flour

8 boneless, skinless chicken breasts, split into halves & pounded ¼" thin with meat hammer

In medium bowl, using wire whisk, or electric mixer on medium speed, combine Club Soda with pancake mix till smooth. Beat in dry mustard & season salt. Set aside. Place flour in shallow bowl. Moisten each piece of chicken breast in water & let excess drip off. Coat lightly but evenly in the flour, placing floured pieces on waxed paper lined surface or cookie sheet until all have been coated. Bring oil to 385F—at least 2-inches deep in electric fry pan or heavy saucepan on top of stove. Spear floured pieces of chicken with tip of sharp knife (do not use tongs!!!)—and dip to coat in prepared batter, letting excess drip back into bowl. Drop few pieces at a time into 385F—oil, frying till golden brown each side, about 4 mins per side. Remove by spearing with tip of knife. Drain on paper toweling. Serve with sauce, at once.

ALMOND CHICKEN SAUCE
Into blender put 14-oz can clear chicken broth, 1 cup water, 3 TB soy sauce, 3 TB cornstarch, pinch sugar. Blend till smooth. Turn into medium saucepan & cook, stirring constantly over medium heat till smooth & thickened. Keep on lowest heat till served.

PREPARE THE ALMONDS for garnishing each serving by melting together in sautee pan, 4 TB butter or margarine & 2 TB oil. Stir in 1 cup thinly sliced almonds. Stir constantly on medium high till almonds turn golden. Remove from heat at once and dump onto paper towels or almonds may quickly burn in their own heat. At once sprinkle the almonds lightly in sugar.

TO SERVE THE ALMOND CHICKEN — Place 2 pieces of fried chicken on each plate and spoon sauce over this. Sprinkle sauteed, sugared almonds over top. Garnish with chopped green onion stems and diced, canned & drained water chestnuts. Serves 8

Gloria Pitzer's MAKE ALIKE RECIPES

Battered Zucchini Slices

Slice unpeeled zuchinni ¼" thick. Moisten in water. Dust in flour. Let dry on waxed paper. With tip of sharp knife spear pieces 1 at time & dip into batter prepared with equal parts Club Soda & dry, boxed pancake mix. Fry in 385F- hot oil few mins each side till brown & crispy.

Shrimp Scampi Sauce

Inspired by the Olive Garden's

½-cup bottled Wishbone Italian Dressing
¼-tsp dry mustard
Few drops Tabasco Sauce
1/3 cup ketchup

With wire whisk combine all ingredients till smooth. Keep refrigerated, tightly covered, to use within a week. Freeze to thaw & use within 4 months. Makes a cup

Seafood Challenge

Shrimp

CRYSTAL SAUCE FOR ORIENTAL
14 LG RAW SHRIMP (20-30-count-per lb.)
½-tsp sugar
1 tsp soy sauce
1½-tsp cornstarch dissolved in 1 TB water
3 TB peanut oil
½-tsp salt
1/3 canned clear chicken broth
 or prepared chicken bouillon
½-cup thinly sliced water chestnuts
1½-cups edible pod peas or 1 pkg frozen pea pods
½-of-a large onion, cut in ½-crosswise, then in
 small wedges
2 short ribs celery cut into ¼" thick slices

Peel shrimp; cut each in half lengthwise by cutting down through rounded backside. Lift out sandy vein. Mix the sugar, soy sauce, cornstarch/water together & heat oil in large skillet or wok to very hot. Add salt & turn shrimp all at once into the pan. Stir & cook for 1 minute or till shrimp turn white & pink. Add broth, water chestnuts, pea pods, onion, celery. Cover & cook 1½-mins. Remove cover once to stir the mixture. Remove cover & add soy sauce, stirring for another few seconds till sauce begins to thicken up & then serve it promptly. Serves 3 to 4 nicely.

Olive Garden

This Oriental Crystal Sauce can also be used with other seafood beside shrimp

Exotic

Gloria Pitzer's MAKE ALIKE RECIPES

SWEET & SOUR SAUCE

If you like the Kraft's Sauce Works Sweet & Sour Sauce, you'll love this!

8-oz can chunk pineapple, undrained
¼-cup orange juice
½-cup cider vinegar
2/3 cup packed brown sugar*
2 TB cornstarch
1 TB dehydrated minced bell peppers
¼-tsp paprika
½-tsp season salt

As listed, put all ingredients, but last 3, into blender, blending high speed about 1 minute till smooth. Pour into 1½-qt saucepan & cook, stirring constantly with wire whisk, med-high heat till smooth & thick. Add last 3 ingredients. Remove from heat. Makes 2 cups.

Plain and simple

JAPANESE BULLDOG SAUCE
(A kind of Worcestershire—but spicier!)

½-cup orange juice
½-cup raisins
¼-cup soy sauce
¼-cup white vinegar
2 TB Dijon mustard (Grey Poupon)
1 TB grated orange peel
2 TB ketchup

Unique

Put all ingredients into 2½-qt saucepan & bring to brisk boil over high, stirring constantly. Reduce heat to gentle simmer & cook stirring only occasionally 5 minutes. Remove from heat. Cool to lukewarm. Funnel into bottle with tight-fitting cap. Refrigerate to use within 6 months. Freeze to thaw and use with a year. Makes 1½-cups sauce.

TERIYAKI SAUCE
Inspired by Lelli's—

¼-cup soy sauce
¼-cup white vinegar
¼-cup ketchup
1 cup orange juice
1 TB Kitchen Bouquet
2 TB melted butter

Combine all ingredients as given, using wire whisk. Refrigerate, tightly covered to use within 30 days. Makes about 2 cups.

Restaurant

SHRIMP COCKTAIL SAUCE

¼-cup ketchup
¼-cup Heinz bottled chili sauce
2 TB pickle relish
2 TB horseradish cream sauce
1 tsp sugar

Combine all ingredients, stirring well & refrigerate tightly covered to use within 30 days. Makes a cup.

JEZABELLE BBQ SAUCE (Pineapple BBQ Sauce)

When the meal is mostly left-overs, dry batter-fried cauliflower buds or mushrooms or chicken tidbits or nuggets with this sauce for a dip.

12-oz jar apple jelly
¼-cup bottled horseradish
12-oz jar pineapple sundae topping
1 tsp dry mustard

Put all 4 ingredients into blender, high speed, about a minute or till smooth. Refrigerate it covered to use within 60 days or freeze to thaw & use within a year. Makes a quart!

BBQ BASTING SAUCE: To 1 cup of Jezabelle Sauce, add 8-oz bottle Catalina Dressing, ¼-cup Heinz 57 Sauce. Use for basting roast chicken, pork or beef.

THOUSAND ISLAND SALAD DRESSING—from Jezabelle Sauce, combine 1 cup Jezabelle Sauce, 1 cup mayonnaise, 1 cup ketchup. Makes 3 cups dressing. Refrigerate to use within 30 days.

SIMPLE!

Gloria Pitzer's MAKE ALIKE RECIPES

109

Sweet & Sour Sauce

7¾-oz jar strained babyfood plums
¼-cup light vinegar —or apricots
½-cup sugar
2 tsp prepared mustard
6 drops Tabasco Sauce

Whip it together with a fork till thoroughly combined. Makes 1½-cups. Keeps if tightly covered and refrigerated up to a month. Freeze the sauce to use within 6 months.

SWEET AND SOUR Pork
(Inspired by Victor Lim's 1950)

Prepare 1 recipe of the Sweet & Sour Sauce and warm it gently in a small saucepan, while you dice enough leftover pork roast into bite-sized pieces, that you have 2 cupsful. Place pork in a 10" skillet and add 14-oz can chicken broth. Simmer gently just to get the pork piping hot and let the pieces of meat loosen-up a bit, so that they are quite soft when touched with a fork. Add a small drained can of water-chestnuts, sliced thin and an 8-oz can drained mushrooms. Scissor snip the stems of 3 green onions into confetti like pieces and stir into the pork mixture. Simmer uncovered, 5 minutes, stirring often. Remove pork and other ingredients, from the broth with a slotted spoon and place in a respectable serving dish. Spoon warm Sweet & Sour Sauce over this. Reserve cooking broth, and use it for preparing rice, to accompany the pork.

PORK SHOULD BE well-done — but never dry. If you use leftover pork roast or pork chops for the above recipe, bring it back to life before combining it with the sauce, by simmering it in a shallow pan with just enough chicken broth to cover it. A good simmering combination, also is to use equal parts chicken broth and tea —spiked with a bit of lemon. For apricot-flavored Sweet & Sour Sauce, substitute babyfood apricots for the plum in above recipe.

Oriental Tempura

1½-cups cornstarch
½-cup flour
2 tsp baking powder
1 tsp season salt
½-tsp lemon-pepper
1 cup Club Soda
1 egg

As listed combine all ingredients, combining with wire whisk till smooth. Let batter stand 5 mins. Moisten foods to be used & coat very lightly but evenly in plain flour & let dry on waxed paper a few mins. Spear pieces of floured food with tip of sharp knife, one at a time & dip to coat in wet batter. Drop into 425F- hot oil, deep enough in pan to let foods "swim" & bob about freely. Fry few mins each side till golden and brown. Remove food with a tip of sharp knife from hot oil. Do not use tongs or coating breaks apart & falls off. Drain food on paper towel-lined baking sheet & keep in 300F-oven till all food has been fried. FOODS TO COAT IN TEMPURA INCLUDE: fresh mushrooms, raw shrimp, sliced, unpeeled zucchini & onions sliced into rings plus frozen, unthawed balls of cheese or chunks of cooked, skinless, boneless chicken.————

TRADITIONAL

Gloria Pitzer's MAKE ALIKE RECIPES

EGGS FOO YUNG

A good lunch dish—or for Sunday breakfast, family-style. The sauce is prepared first, since the eggs should not have to stand, once they are completed, or they become dry and tough. The ingredients you choose —like your mileage—may vary. The basic egg mixture is prepared like a scrambled egg mixture, without stirring it in the skillet, so that it cooks like a pancake. But do not turn it. The top should be slightly soft and only the edges a bit dry. Then you sprinkle on the ingredients of your choice—or those we recommend below—and fold the egg in half, slipping it onto a heated serving platter. To heat it quickly, run it under hot tap water & dry it off. Spray it then with a whisper of Pam to keep the egg from sticking. You spoon the sauce over the folded egg and cut it into wedges to serve to 3 or 4 very nicely!

13¾-oz (approx) can clear chicken broth
2 TB cornstarch
1 TB soy sauce
1 TB margarine or butter
A few flecks of parsley flakes

6 eggs
2 TB water
½-tsp onion powder

small can drained, sliced water chestnuts
2 or 3 green onion stems, scissor-snipped
1-lb can drained bean sprouts, snipped fine

Put chicken broth, cornstarch & soy sauce into blender on high speed about half a minute or till smooth. Pour into small saucepan. On high to med-high, stir constantly till thickened & just comes to boil. Remove from heat at once. Stir in the 1 TB margarine or butter & parsley flakes. Set this aside. Put the eggs, water & onion powder through blender till smooth. Melt just enough butter or margarine to coat bottom of 12" Teflon-coated or copper-bottom Rever ware skillet. Pour in egg mixture and cook without stirring, on med-high, just till edges appear dry and top is almost "set". Remove from heat. Sprinkle remaining ingredients over surface of egg. Fold in half to cover ingredients. Slip onto heated serving platter. Spoon warm sauce over egg. Cut into wedges to serve 4. (Leftovers do not keep well.)

OPTIONAL INGREDIENTS:

You may use in addition to the above suggested ingredients, or in place of them:

8-oz can drained mushrooms, well diced
8-oz pkg frozen cooked baby shrimp, thawed & drained
1 cup leftover diced pork roast—no fat or gristle
6 slices bacon fried crispy and crumbled

The egg mixture may be cut in half—for two generous servings, adjusting additonal ingredients for topping, of course. The sauce recipe should not be cut in half, but can be doubled or tripled. It can be refrigerated in covered container to be rewarmed within a week. Do not freeze the sauce, however.

THE SAUCE for the Eggs Foo Yung is also the basis for preparing a gravy for Shrimp Chow Mein or Chop Suey. The ingredients are altered just a bit, but then so are most famous dishes created from a basic recipe that can be used for many different dishes. I like this sauce because you only have to remember the 3 basic ingredients, and the addition of the butter and parsley flakes is just to give it character!

SHRIMP CHOW MEIN

2 cans (13¾-oz approx. each) clear chicken broth
4 TB cornstarch (level measure)
2 TB soy sauce
2 TB butter or margarine
½-tsp dry parsley flakes

1-lb bag frozen, cooked baby shrimp, thawed
small can sliced water chestnuts, well drained
1-lb can bean sprouts, drained
8-oz can mushrooms, drained
13¾-oz can clear chicken broth

Put the 2 cans chicken broth into blender with cornstarch & soy sauce. Blend on high speed ½-min till smooth. Pour into 2-qt saucepan & cook & stir constantly over high heat till it just comes to boil. Drop in butter and sprinkle on parsley flakes. Give it a stir or two & let it stand while you put the well drained shrimp & remaining ingredients into another accomodating pan to heat it—only till piping hot. Pour the blender-mixture sauce into heated ingredient mixture. Spoon over canned Chow Mein noodles in individual serving dishes to accomodate 4—or spoon the mixture over cooked, hot, fluffed Uncle Ben's long grain rice. Serve with soy sauce on the side. Do not freeze leftover, but you may refrigerate them, well covered, to rewarm within a few days.

PORK CHOP SUEY

Prepare the sauce as given above for the Shrimp Chow Mein, and set it aside. Meanwhile cut up enough leftover pork roast lean meat to yield 2 cups bite-sized pieces. Place in shallow skillet with 14-oz can clear chicken broth and simmer about 5 mins or till piping hot. Stir in the prepared blender-mixture sauce and add, if you wish the water chestnuts, bean sprouts, drained mushrooms as recommended in above recipe, keeping mixture warm until ready to serve over hot cooked rice. Serves 4 nicely.

SHRIMP FRIED RICE

Prepare enough Uncle Ben's long grain rice, per box directions to give you 2 cups cooked rice. Melt 4 TB margarine & 4 TB oil in 12" skillet. Add drained, almost dry cooked rice, stirring it on low heat till coated in oil mixture. Keep on lowest heat while adding an 8-oz bag frozen cooked baby shrimp, thawed & drained well, 4 green onion stems, scissor-snipped quite fine, 3 TB soy sauce. Transfer to greased 2-qt baking dish to serve as an accompiment to Chow Mein dishes. Serves 4 to 6. Refrigerate leftovers to use in a week. Do not freeze!

Gloria Pitzer's MAKE ALIKE RECIPES

HOW TO MAKE YOUR OWN EASTER EGG DYE

You can hard boil the eggs in beet juice & half as much water to obtain a pink color. Without water - just beet juice, you achieve a deeper shade of red. Putting fresh parsley leaves through the blender with only enough water to give the parsley "swimming room" and then blending on high speed till minced, you can produce a green color when you boil the eggs in this mixture. Yellow colored eggs can be achieved by adding 1 or 2 tablespoons ground turmeric to a quart of water in which you would boil eggs. OR for a more golden color remove the outer yellow skins of whole onions and boil these with the eggs, allowing the skins of 4 onions for 1-qt water. Purple is achieved by boiling the eggs in dark grape juice or by putting a 15-oz can blueberries, undrained, into blender on high speed till pureed and adding half as much water in which to boil eggs.

HOW TO PROPERLY BOIL EGGS

Arrange eggs close together in deep saucepan & add enough cold water to cold eggs, gradually. To keep eggs from rocking around during cooking, place metal measuring cups of varying sizes between any spaces to keep eggs snuggly together and in place. Water level should be at least 2" above surface of eggs, keeping eggs in single layer. Bring to a boil. Turn heat down to keep water barely simmering for **8 minutes** & then turn off heat. Cover pan with lid & allow to stand till water is lukewarm. Keep eggs refrigerated, preferably in covered container so egg odor does not affect other foods. **TO PEEL EGGS** begin with cold tap water running. Tap wide end of egg on hard surface to crack-almost gently smashing the area of the shell-allowing then cold water to run over the egg as you begin to remove peel, letting water seep into egg ythrough the cracked end. This helps to loosen entire shell & let the shell come easily away from the egg. Keep peeled eggs refrigerated in tightly covered container to use within 24 hours. Eggs, hard boiled & in the shell will keep refrigerated one week. Do not freeze please.

PICKLED EGGS

Refrigerate peeled hard boiled eggs in pickled beet juice with beets & sliced onions, a week, tightly covered.

Cooking up an Easter

Gloria Pitzer's MAKE ALIKE RECIPES

Every Christmas while the children were growing up I would decorate a candy house for them. It was entirely edible and always a welcomed tradition in our house.

the Christmas season
CANDY HOUSE

Ingredients:
- ¼-cup cornstarch
- 4-lbs powdered sugar
- Food Colorings assorted
- ¾-cup hot water
- 1 TB almond extract
- Assorted hard candied Necco wafer candies
- A few pointed end ice cream cones to use (inverted) for pine trees
- Large green gum drops for shrubs

Blend all ingredients together, adding water little at a time to give the mixture a spreading consistency, beating in extract also. Beat till very smooth. Place in top of double boiler over gently simmering water just to keep frosting mixture warm. Stir it frequently to keep from caking around sides of pan. Spread it over entire surface of a thick cardboard box that measures about 8x10-inches on two sides and about 4x6-inches on the other two sides. (A large shoe box will do!) Cut a rectangle of similar strength cardboard, creasing it in center to bend (poster board works well), for the roof as shown in drawing above. The roof will be attached to the box with masking tape, holding it securely in place. Do likewise with two triangular pieces of cardboard to fill in the ends of the roof. After taping it well together place it on a foil-covered tray or cookie sheet. Secure sides to foil with more masking tape, which you will be covering with the prepared frosting mixture, so the tape will not be showing. Dab a little icing on bottom of box to keep it from slipping around, then coat it completely with thin layer of the icing. Work quickly. Place hard Christmas candies on iced surface with additional icing for windows and doors and shutters. Use square candy for windows, or oval shapes, rectangle shapes for shutters and the waffle cut candies in rows for the door. Let icing drip over roof edge to look like snow and icicles.

THE ROOF will be made with Necco Wafer candies, overlapping them row-by-row beginning with the lower edge of roof at top of house and working up to top of roof, where it is creased. Apply as much frosting to the Necco candies as needed to make them stick well in place. If a little of the icing appears to ooze out between candies, don't worry. It will appear to look like snow when all is said and done. The cornstarch in the frosting mixture should help it to dry quickly. Egg whites can be slightly beaten and also worked into the frosting to give it more of a shine and cause it to also dry more quickly, if you wish. Use about 1 egg white for every TWO cups of prepared frosting. Inverted ice cream cones can be frosted with green tinted frosting for pine trees and these can be placed around the sides of the house. Large green gumdrops will make nice shrubs as well as small lollipops with the sticks inserted into gum drops for additional landscaping.

Gloria Pitzer's MAKE ALIKE RECIPES

FRESH CRANBERRY SAUCE

1½-cups water
1½-cups sugar   12-oz bag fresh cranberries

In 2½-qt saucepan combine water & sugar. Bring to boil and boil rapidly 3 mins. Add cranberries. Stir often on med-hi heat. Cook then on gentle simmer 10 mins or till berry skins "pop". Turn heat to lowest point, cooking till few drops of sauce, dropped onto cold plate, gels quickly. Refrigerate covered, to use within 2 wks. Freeze to use in 6 months. (Makes about 2½-cups sauce).

FRESH PUMPKIN - Baked
Inspired by Libby's canned pumpkin

Scrub pumpkin thoroughly. Cut into halves or quarters, depending on size. Remove seeds & stringy parts & place skin-side-up in shallow roasting pan with 1/4" water in it. Bake covered loosely with foil at 400F- about 1 hr or till fork tender. Let cool & scrape meaty part away from skin. Mash well or put through blender or food processor & pack in freezer containers, leaving 1" headspace. Seal lids in masking tape. Date to thaw & use in 6 months. (Apple cider can be used in place of water in pan for better flavor.) Allow 2 cups mashed pumpkin to replace 1-lb can of pumpkin.

CHRISTMAS DIVINITY Just Like The Royal Oak Sweet Shop 1947

This recipe came from our friends John and Avis Cobb of Marysville (Mich) and when I first sampled this wonderful candy, I immediately thought of The Sweet Shop on Main Street in Royal Oak, after the war, when we could stop there on our way home from a Saturday matinee at The Main Theater. Usually I would spend my quarter on a few pieces of Divinity and a few pieces of fudge. Here is a memory!

Beat 2 egg whites stiff but not dry; set aside. In a heavy 2½-qt saucepan, bring to a boil, 2½-cups sugar, ½-cup light corn syrup, ½-cup water, cooking this to the "soft-ball stage". (When a little dropped from a teaspoon into a glass of cold water, the candy will form a soft ball on the bottom of the glass. If it looks like pollywogs however, it needs a bit more cooking!) At the soft ball stage, remove candy from heat. Beat in ½-tsp vanilla, using electric mixer on med-high speed and beat HALF of the candy mixture into the egg whites that you earlier set aside. The remaining half of the candy, still in the saucepan must then be returned to the heat to cook to the "hard carck" stage — when a small amount dropped from a spoon into a glass of cold water, the candy mixture will actually "crack" or snap when it hits the water. Then working quickly, beat the hot candy mixture into egg white mixture, beating on high speed till mixture has lost its shine. Stir in 2 cups of chopped walnuts or pecans. Quickly drop mixture by teaspoonful onto greased waxed paper lined cookie sheets. Let dry at room temperature. Makes 4 to 5 dozen.

Gloria Pitzer's MAKE ALIKE RECIPES

HEART SHAPED CAKE

for Valentine's Day

Special Recipe

Preparing a boxed 18-oz cake mix as the package directs, I'll bake one layer in an 8" round pan & one in an 8" square pan. Arrange the square layer so that facing you on a foil-covered pizza pan, it looks like a diamond. Cut the round layer in half & arrange cut sides against 2 sides of square layer—as in photo at right! Seal cut sides with frosting. Garnish with M&M candies turning plain side of each candy UP —as shown.

Sugar Plums

The "visions of sugar plums" that danced in the heads of the children in the beloved Christmas verse, "A Visit From St. Nicholas" were in no way —shape or form, related to plums, but were sweet confections popular in the last century in England. A candy concoction that was created by English cooks from a mixture of sugar, fruits, nuts and porridge to hold it together, would not appeal to many lovers of candies today. We have updated this traditional Christmas treat by using only 4 ingredients.

Modern Sugar Plums

Empty a 1-lb container of ready-to-spread vanilla frosting into a 2½-qt oven-proof bowl & Micro melt it on medium for 2 minutes—OR put the frosting into top of double boiler over simmering water till melted & hot. Then remove from heat & stir in 2 cups flaked coconut, 8-oz pkg chopped walnuts and 1½-cups light raisins. Pack mixture evenly in greased 8" or 9" square pan. Cover in plastic wrap & refrigerate 1 hour. Cut into 36 squares. Keep refrigerated to serve in 30 days. Makes 36 pieces.

MINCEMEAT HOMEMADE

1-lb pitted dates
1½-cup Coca-Cola or Pepsi
1 cup orange marmalade
1 cup dark raisins
¼-tsp salt

Bring mixture to boil in 2-qt saucepan. Reduce to simmer, stirring frequently till thickened. Turn off heat and stir in:

1 tsp cinnamon
½-tsp nutmeg
2 cups chopped walnuts
2 cups peeled, cored, grated apples
2 cups finely diced, cooked roast beef or pork roast
½-cup whiskey or brandy (or two 1-oz bottles flavor)
9-oz can undrained crushed pineapple
½-cup melted butter

Keep refrigerated in covered container up to 2 weeks or prepare & freeze up to 6 months.

TO USE AS PIE FILLING:
Combine 2½-c mincemeat
½-cup flour
¼-c butter melted

Spread evenly over bottom of pastry-lined 9" pie pan. Add top crust. Flute to seal rims & make slits to allow steam to escape during baking. Brush crust with 2 TB soft butter & dust in 1 tsp sugar. Bake 375 degrees—30-35 mins or till golden brown. Serves 6-8.

Gloria Pitzer's MAKE ALIKE RECIPES

RIGHT AWAY FROSTED FRUITCAKE

Make this fruitcake up in the afternoon & serve it that evening!

- 1-lb candied cherries - whole
- 10-oz pkg pitted dates, cut up small
- 1 cup golden or light raisins
- 1 cup chopped pecans or walnuts
- 18-oz box yellow cake mix
- 20-oz can apple pie filling
- 3 large eggs
- 1 TB cinnamon

Put 6 of the candied cherries aside to use as garnish later. Mix the rest of the cherries with the dates, raisins, nuts & dry cake mix, right from the box, coating every single piece in the cake mix powder. Put last 3 ingredients into blender. Blend high speed, ½-minute just to combine well like a sauce. Pour blender mixture over cake mix mixture, stirring well with large spoon to moisten every bit of it. Press any dry particles with back of spoon to moisten & then pack batter into Pam-sprayed or greased & floured 10-inch tube pan or Bundt pan. Bake at 350F—for 1 hour & 10 mins or till a tester inserted into cake comes out clean. Cool upright in pan on rack 1 hour. Loosen edges of cake with tip of sharp knife & invert onto platter. Glaze with this frosting:

FRUITCAKE FROSTING— Into 1½-qt saucepan put following ingredients: ½-cup packed light brown sugar, 6 TB orange juice. Stir on high, bringing it to boil. Simmer gently 2 mins, stirring constantly. Remove from heat. Beat in 2 cups powdered sugar & 1 tsp orange or vanilla extract, using electric mixer on high speed till smooth. Drizzle the frosting artistically over the top of cake, letting it drip down the sides. Arrange candied cherries on top as garnish and sprinkle in additonal nuts if you wish. Slice to serve right away! Refrigerate leftovers to use in 2 weeks.

FRUITCAKE

1991 holiday Christmas

NO BAKE FRUITCAKE

- 4 cups fine Graham cracker crumbs (about 4 dozen 2½" square crackers)
- 1 cup mixed candied fruit
- 1 cup golden raisins
- 1 cup chopped dates
- 1 cup chopped walnuts
- 1 cup mini marshmallows
- 14-oz can Eagle Brand Milk

Line a greased 9" bread-loaf pan in waxed paper & grease the paper. Mix all ingredients well, first using a sturdy spoon, then get your hands into the mixture, combining it thoroughly. When every dry particle is completely moistened pack mixture well into prepared pan. Seal in Seran Wrap. Refrigerate at least 24 hrs— better for 48 hours, before serving, sliced into 1" thick slices & garnished in hard sauce or whipped cream. OR you may cut into slices & then into small squares to serve from a platter like you would cookies. Makes 2-lb fruitcake..

EAGLE BRAND FRUITCAKE

- 2½-cups flour
- 1 tsp baking soda
- 2 eggs, slightly beaten
- 2-2/3 cups mincemeat (28-oz jar None-Such)
- 14-oz can Eagle Brand Milk
- 2 cups (1-lb) mixed candied fruits
- 1 cup chopped walnuts or pecans
- Candied Cherries for garnishing

Mix flour & soda & set aside. In mixing bowl combine eggs, mincemeat, canned milk, fruit & nuts. Work in flour mixture. When every single dry particle has been moistened, transfer to greased & floured 10" Bundt pan. Bake almost 2 hours (1 hour plus 50 mins) in a preheated 300F oven—or until a tester inserted through center of baked portion of cake comes out clean. (Tester to use is a paper-covered wire trash bag "twist".) Cool in pan 15 mins on wire rack. Remove cake from pan carefully to platter & garnish in cherries. Drizzle with a little clear corn syrup to give a nice glazed look. Refrigerate cake tightly covered in plastic container to serve within 2 weeks or freeze to thaw and serve within 6 months.

Gloria Pitzer's MAKE ALIKE RECIPES

INDEX

- Alfredo Sauce-95
- Alibi Inn Style Dressing-57
- All-Purpose Salad Dressing-57
- Almond Chicken-106
- Almonds For Garnish-106
- American Fries-79
- Apple Cobbler-36
- Apple Muffins-13
- Apple Pancake-18
- Apple Struedel-22
- Applettes-17
- Applettes-17
- Apricot Sauce Oriental-109
- Archway Imitations-17, 36
- Au Jus Gravy-86
- Bacon Properly Prepared-96
- Baked Beans-78
- Baked Pecan halves-21
- Baking Powder Biscuits-15
- Barbecue Basting Jezabelle-108
- Barbecue Beef Sandwich-87
- Barbecued Ribs-91
- Barbecue Sauce-56
- Barbecue Sauce (Hedges')-87
- Barbecue Sauce (Kraft's)-56
- Barbecue Sauce (Steak Ale)-56
- Barbecue Sauce (Texas)-63
- Basting Broth For Fish-103
- Batter Bread-19
- Battered Zucchini-107
- Bean Soup (Bill Knapp)-74
- Bean Soup (Buggy Works)-76
- Bearnaise Sauce-63
- Beef Roasts-83
- Beef Soup-70, 71
- Beef Tips-86
- Belgian Waffle-30
- Big Boy Inspired Tom Dress-60
- " " Oatmeal Cookies-36, 44
- Bill Knapp Biscuit Rolls-9
- Bill Knapp Zucchini Bread-34
- Bird's Eye Inspired Sauces-62
- Biscuits (Popeye/Hardee's)-15
- Biscuits (Bill Knapp Style)-9
- Black Bean Soup-74
- Black Eyed Pea Soup-74
- Blender Icing-13
- Blizzard Imitation-43
- Bob Evans Inspired Noodles-94
- " " Vegetable Soup-70
- Boboli Imitation-91
- Bologna Salad-90
- Boston Clam Chowder-69
- Breadsticks-8, 9
- Bread Without Yeast-19
- Broccoli Soup (Big Boy)-72
- Broiling Steaks-85
- Buffalo Wings-93
- Buggy Works Salad Imitation-76
- Bulldog Sauce-108
- Bundt Cake (From Scratch)-39
- Buttercream Without Butter-38
- Butter Crust Pie Crust-35
- Buttermilk fudge Cake-31
- Butterscotch Topping-47
- Cabbage Soup Ala Deli-73
- Caesar Dressing/Red Lobster-57
- Candy House Directions-113
- Caramel Cookies-35
- Caramel Icing-24
- Cashew Nougat Cookies-36
- Catfish Oven Style-103
- Cathy Cheesecake Imitation-22
- Catsup-67
- Cheese Biscuits-6
- Cheesecake NY-22/Sugar-Free-27
- Cheese Frenchies-98
- Cheese Sauce-98
- Cheese Soup (Denny's)-74
- Cheese Wish-66
- Chi Chi Inspired Dressing-52
- Chicken Broth Concentrate-68
-     From Scratch-77
- Chicken Fajita McFabulous-105
- Chicken Gravy-80
- Chicken & Noodles-94
- Chicken Pot Pie-80
- Chicken Salad-52
- Chicken Shredded-90
- Chicken Soup-75
- Chicken This Evening Sauce-72
- Chicken Wings-93
- Chili - Green Chili-103
-     Like Hormel's-102
-     Like Steak & Ale's-102
-     Like Lafayette's-102
- Chimichanga Gravy (Chi Chi)-103
- Chinese Egg Rolls-104
- Chip In The Middle Imitation-21
- Chocolate Cake-37
- Chocolate Chip Ala Big Boy-44
- Chocolate Chip Ala Sanders-44
- Chocolate Chunk Cookies-21, 26
- Chocolate Cupcakes-20
- Chocolate Gravy-19
- Chocolate Ice Cream-48
- Chocolate Mousse Pie-18
- Chow Mein-111
- Christmas Recipes-113-116
- Cinnamon Bread Ala HoJo-7
- Clam Chowder-69 Sauce-100
- Coffee Can Ice Cream-48
- Cole Slaw Ala Suzie Q-53
- Coleslaw Ala Long John's-52

Iorla Pitzer's MAKE ALIKE RECIPES

INDEX

- Coney Island Sauce-102
- Cookie Sheet Preparation-17, 43
- Corn Pudding-80
- Corn Souffle-80
- Cream Filling-24, 28
- Cream Broccoli Soup-72
- Cream Tomato Soup-75
- Cream Puff Filling-28
- Cream Sauce For Chicken-72
- Creamy Ceasar-55
- Creamy Garlic-58, 77
- Cranberry Sauce/scratch-114
- Crazy Bread-8
- Crumb Cake-39
- Custard, cooked-49
- Date Bars-42
- Deli Cabbage Soup-73
- Denny Style Cheese Soup-74
- Dessert Pizza-27
- Devil Dogs (Whoopie Pie)-24
- Dijon Mustard-78
- Dill Pickles-Voyageur-57
- Dirty Rice-Popeye-73
- Divinity-114
- Donut Fillings-28
- Durkee Sauce Imitation-56
- Eagle Brand Fruitcake-116
- Easter Egg Dye-112
- Eggnog-49
- Eggplant Parmesan-99
- Egg Rolls-104
- Egg Foo Yung-110
- Eggs Properly Boiled-112
- Elephant Ears-20
- Escalloped Apples-17
- Fajita-105
- Famous Durkee Imitation-56
- FarmerJack Rice Salad-60
- Fat Free Dressing-51, 57
- Fat Free Pie-34 Ice Cream-45
- Fat Free Soup-71
- Fig New Funs-42
- Fillet Mignon Marinade-86
- Fine Herbs-55
- Fish-Broiled-106, Smoked-64
- Flat Bread Pizza-8
- Fogcutter Dressing-51
- Frajita Fries-88
- Frankenmuth Bread-16/Stollen-16
- French Blue Cheese-77
- French Dressing-51
- French Fries-88/Seasoning-61
- French Silk Pies-36
- Fried Rice-111
- Friendship Cake Starter-10
- Fruit Snack-17
- Frosting-Wedding Cake-50
- Frosting Mix-Coconut/Pecan-23
- Frozen Yogurt-46
- Fruitcakes-116
- Fudge cake-30, 31
- Fudge-Mamie Eisenhower's-40
- Fudge Special Frosting-37
- Garden Soup-71
- Garlic Cheese Biscuits-6
- Girl Scout Imitations-25, 35
- Glorified Rice-60
- Good Reasons-59
- Good Samaritan-12
- Goody Goody Hamburger Sauce-61
- Grapenuts-7
- Gravy-80, 86
- Green Chili-103
- Ham BBQ-92, Salad-90, Croquettes-93, Fresh-92
- Hardly's Mushroom Sauce-61
- Hash Brown Casserole-79
- Heart Shaped Cake-115
- Hedges' Recipes-51, 87
- Herman-11
- Hollandaise-63
- Honey Mustard-55, 57, 61, 63
- Horn Mill Chili-102
- Hudson Clam Sauce-100
- Ice Box Pizza Dough-8
- Ice Cream Cones-47
- Italian Dressing Mix-59
  - Shortbread Cookies-44
  - Wedding Cake-50
- Japanese Bulldog Sauce-108
  - Sauce Ala Birds'Eye-62
- Jelly Donuts-29
- Jezabelle BBQ Sauce-108
- Jimmy Launce Inspired Soup-71
- Ketchup.Like Brooks'-67
- Key Lime Pie
  - like Red Lobster-34
- Lasagna like Roma Hall's-96
- Lafayette Chili Imitation-102
- Lelli's Inspired
  - Recipes-86, 108

Gloria Pitzer's MAKE ALIKE RECIPES

INDEX

Lelli's Teriyaki-108
Lelli's Marinade-86
Lemon Blender Icing-27
Lemonade Homemade-49
Lemon Layer Cake-31
Lemon Pie-33
Lemon Poppyseed Muffins-13
Lemon sorbet-47
Lentil Soup-74
Macaroni/Cheese-Beef Carver-95
Mama's In A Minute Cake-15
Mamie Eisenhower's Fudge-40
Marinade for Beef Steaks-84
Marinade For Chicken-95
Marinated Chicken (YaYa)-98
Marty's Salad Imitation-76
Mary Ann Frosted Cookies-17
Marzesty Slaw Dressing-59
Mashed Potatoes-81
McFabulous Fajitas-105
   Honey Mustard Sauce-61
   Muffins-13
   Oriental Dressing-54
Meatloaf ala Beef Carver-87
Mexican Seasoning-105
Milano Cookie Imitation-42
Milky Way Cake-39
Mincemeat Homemade-115
Mint Cookies Ala Girl Scout-26
Mint Milano Cookies-42
Muer's Martha Salad-81
   Breadsticks-8
   Spaghetti Sauce-97
Mushroom Sauce (Hardee)-61
Mustard Sauce-56
Nest Leased Crunch Bars-40
New England Sauce (Bird's)-62
No Bake Fruitcake-116
Noodles Alfredo-95
Noodles/Pasta Homemade-101
No Rolling Pin Pie Crust-35
No Yolk Mayonnaise-59
Oatmeal Raisin Cookies-36
   Ala Hudson's-26
Olga Bread-14
Olive Garden Inspired
   Dressing-34/Eggplant-99
     Mousse Pie-18/Sauce-107
   Soup-70
Onion Blossom-89
Onion Ring Loaf-89/Bracelets-89
Onion Soup-69/Swiss Style-70
Orange Nut Bread-Knapp's-37
Oriental Dressing-54

Oven Pancake (IHOP)-18
Oyster Stuffing-94
Paczki (Punch Keys)-29
Parmesan Dressing-54
Party Smoked Ham-92
Pasta Dough-101
Pasta Fagioli-70
Pasta Primavera (Muer)-101
Pastry Horn Cream Filling-28
Peanut Soup-69
Pettit Fours-20
Picante Sauce-56
Picled Beets-53
Pickled Eggs-112
Pie Crust-35
Pierogies-97
Pineapple Jezabelle-108
Pineapple (KTOK) Cake-15
Pineapple Pie-32
Pizza Crust-91
Pizza Make Ahead Dough-8
Pizza Roll Sauce-104/Rolls-104
Pizza Style Flat Bread-8
Plum Sauce-109
Ponderosa Inspired Dressing-54
Poppyseed Muffins-13
Poppyseed Dressing-55
Pork Chop Suey-111
Pork Roast-92 POT ROAST-86
Potato Chip Cookies-49
Potato Salad-58, 81
Potato Skins-79
Potato Soup/baked potatoes-79
Potato Sourdough Starter-10
Potatoes Make Ahead-79
Potpourri Homemade-65
Pot Roast-85, Marinade-86
Poundcake-Powdered Sugar-50
Prime Rib-83
Pumpkin/Fresh Baked-114
Pumpkin Seeds Salty-38
Punch Key Polish Donuts-29
Raisin Bread-10/Sourdough-12
Ram's Horn Inspired Quiche-82
RANCH DRESSING MIX (dry)-58
Raspberry Pie-32/Vinagrette-81
Red Lob Inspired tartar sauce-62
   Dressing-57/rolls-6
Rib Rub For Spareribs-91
Rice Confetti (Farmer Jack)-60
Rice Pudding/Cream of Wheat/-30
Right Away Fruitcake-116
Roast Beef-83
Roma Hall Lasagna-96
Salad Supreme Imitation-63
Salsa-56
Sanders Chocolate Cupcakes-20

Gloria Pitzer's MAKE ALIKE RECIPES

Sandwich Cookie/Girl Scout-26
San Francisco Sourdough-11
Sauce For Almond Chicken-106
Sauce For Pizza Rolls-104
Scalloped Apples-17
Scalloped Potatoes-78
Schlotzsky Imitation Rolls-14
Seafood Pasta Salad-51
Seasoned French Fries-88
Self Rising Flour-9
Sherbet (Sorbet)-47
Shoney Imitation Fudgecake-30
Shredded Chicken-90
Shrimp Chow mein-111
Shrimp Cocktail Sauce-107, 108
Shrimp Fried Rice-111
Shrimp Scampi Sauce-111
Simmering Potpourri-65
Slaw Dressing-53
Slow Cooker Beef Roast-86
Smoked Salmon-64
Smoking Fish At Home-64
Snickers Bar Cake-39/Candy-41
Snow Cones-45
Snowstorm Blizzard-43
SOFT OATMEAL COOKIES-26
Soup From Scratch-77
Sour Cream Homemade-64
Sourdough Biscuits-11
Sourdough Starter-11
Sour Milk-37
Sour Milk Fudgecake-37
Spaghetti Salad (Ponderosa)-51
Spaghetti Sauce like Muer-97
Spaghetti Sauce/tomatoes-100
Spaghetti Sauce/grape jelly-100
Spaghetti Shrimp Salad-53
Spanish Rice like Chi Chi-103
Spareribs-91
Special Sanders Frosting-37
Spoice Cake Mix-23
Spice Cookies-Frosted-17
Spinach like Joe Muer's-82
Spinach Quiche-82
Split Pea Soup-74
Standing Rib Roast-83
STARTER RECIPES-10
Steak & Shake Imitation -102
Steak Marinade-84
Steaks-broiled-seared,etc-84
Steak Sauce-86
Stewed Tomatoes-68
Strawberry Candies-40
Strawberry Ice Cream-48
Strawberry Jam-67

Strawberry Leather-19
Strawberry Pie-32
Streussel Crust-35
Stuffing-94
SUGAR FREE BUTTERCREAM-38
    Cheesecake-27
    Chocolate Cookies-49
    Feathery Fudge Cake-38
    Frozen Custard-45
    Ketchup-68
    Lemon Pie-33
    Peach Ice Cream-46
    Pineapple Pie-32
    Raspberry Pie-32
    Sweet Pickles-65
Sugar Plums-115
Summer Soup-72
Suzie Q Slaw-53
Sweet & Sour Pork-109
Sweet & Sour Salad Dressing-76
Sweet & Sour Sauce-108, 109
Sweeten House Rice-60
Sweet Pickles out of Dill-65
Swiss Onion Soup-70
Taco Bell style meat-105
Tartar Sauce like Red Lob-62
Tempura-109
Teriyaki Sauce-108
Thin Vanilla Glaze-12
Thousand Island Jezabelle-108
Three-in-one Dressing-58
Tomato Florentine Soup-73
Tomato Spice (Big Boy)-60
Tomato Soup-77
Tuna Noodle Casserole-94
Tuna Twix Mix-60
Twice Baked Potatoes-88
Valentine Cake-115
Vanilla Blender Icing-13
Vanilla Extract-66
Vanilla Glaze-12
Veg Soup like Bob Evans'-70
Veg Soup (Jimmy Launce)-71
Velvet Cheese Loaf-66
Vinagrette-52
Vinegar Homemade-55
Voyageur Imitations-57
Wedding Cake-50
White Cake Mix-23
White Pizza-99
White Sauce-93
Whole Wheat Bread-6
Whoopie Pies-24
Yogurt Homemade-46